T0196088

Ask the Psychic Medium

Bonnie Page

BALBOA.
PRESS

A DIVISION OF HAY HOUSE

Copyright © 2019 Bonnie Page.

All rights reserved. No part of this book may be used or reproduced by any means, graphic, electronic, or mechanical, including photocopying, recording, taping or by any information storage retrieval system without the written permission of the author except in the case of brief quotations embodied in critical articles and reviews.

Balboa Press books may be ordered through booksellers or by contacting:

Balboa Press
A Division of Hay House
1663 Liberty Drive
Bloomington, IN 47403
www.balboapress.com
1 (877) 407-4847

Because of the dynamic nature of the Internet, any web addresses or links contained in this book may have changed since publication and may no longer be valid. The views expressed in this work are solely those of the author and do not necessarily reflect the views of the publisher, and the publisher hereby disclaims any responsibility for them.

The author of this book does not dispense medical advice or prescribe the use of any technique as a form of treatment for physical, emotional, or medical problems without the advice of a physician, either directly or indirectly. The intent of the author is only to offer information of a general nature to help you in your quest for emotional and spiritual well-being. In the event you use any of the information in this book for yourself, which is your constitutional right, the author and the publisher assume no responsibility for your actions.

Any people depicted in stock imagery provided by Getty Images are models, and such images are being used for illustrative purposes only.
Certain stock imagery © Getty Images.

Print information available on the last page.

ISBN: 978-1-9822-1889-8 (sc)
ISBN: 978-1-9822-1890-4 (e)

Balboa Press rev. date: 01/07/2019

Contents

In The Beginning – My Beginning That Is:

I was born into a family of spiritualists. For many generations, my ancestors have had this gift from God running through their veins. I was often told that my grandmother and great-grandmother on my mother's side of the family were so gifted that they could make a broom walk across the floor or make spoons bend. Well, that's just a little bit freaky if you ask me, but to this day whenever I look at my own broom, I'll say to it "if you're gonna move, you better start sweeping"! That being said, I've seen spirit and spirit animals ever since I can remember back to about the age of four.

I grew up in a small, rural town in New England. The house I grew up in was an old, historical schoolhouse where children learned in one big room, and there always seemed to be spirits available for my viewing. You know how children will sometimes have imaginary friends – well I seemed to have many! I had one special friend in particular who would actually follow me outside to play. The little girl with the straight brown hair and bangs was always there in the times when I needed her. Later in life, describing her to my mother, I was told she was here many years before.

There always seemed to be somebody from spirit there watching and guiding me, such as a Native American who would sit on the porch and wait for me to get off the bus every day from school. My mom could see what I was seeing and would reassure me that he was one of my guides watching to make sure I got home safely every day. I always felt loved and protected.

The only time my gift was or could be a little bit scary was in the middle of the night when I could sense and see spirit around me. I slept with a full light on until the age of 14 and couldn't fall asleep unless I could hear my dad snoring in the next room. I know now that when it's your sleep time or dream time that the veil is at its thinnest, making it easier for spirits to get their message through. As I grew up, I would awaken up every morning around 3:00, the spiritual hour, and I would get up and have a cup of tea. My mom used to always tell me "you've gotta be scared of the living – the dead aren't going to hurt you." Okay, mom, I believe you, but that still doesn't help me to sleep at night!

Recently, I met a group of friends from high school. We all got together for dinner, and I was asked the question "could you see things back then?" "Of course I could," I replied. They continued to ask, "but why didn't you ever tell us?" Can you just imagine walking down the halls of your high school and telling people you can see dead people? I'm pretty sure no one would have asked me to the prom!

So, I lived my life like most people do, enjoying everything that went along with it – marriage, having a baby, a career. And to most people, my life seemed quite normal. But I was always taking in the guidance that was still being sent down to me from heaven, many times hearing the voice of God, as he always called me "little one."

I still didn't talk about it with most people, except my mom, who was my biggest confidant. And since she had these same gifts, it was nice to be able to talk to her about the things that would happen. My mom always understood.

I loved being guided, then there came a time when my son joined the Army, and my husband was working a lot of hours that the signs started to appear of how my life was about to change. God waits for just the right time to make his message known. God and spirit started sending me down a new path.

As I was mechanically putting on my makeup one day, I heard God's voice coming through loud and clear. "I need you to do more of this work (God's work) for me," and I said "why?" and he said, "because the world is becoming a darker & darker place and we need more light." I owned a salon at the time, and I asked, "God, what if I starve?" and he answered back "have I ever let you starve?" And it's true – I had never starved or wanted. God always gave me what I needed.

As I walked into the living room and told my husband George "God wants me to do my mediumship full-time," he responded, "then do it!"

With his blessings and support, Messages From Heaven was born - a healing and learning center for me to bring healing messages to those in need and teach others how to get in touch with their own abilities.

After my conversation with God, I went to train with some of the most renowned psychic mediums in the US and the UK to hone my gifts and to bring spirit in stronger. Messages from Heaven is a three-way conversation; From spirit, Through spirit, and To spirit. I feel inspired to do God's work by comforting those who need to hear from their loved ones on the other side. I have developed an enhanced ability to see, hear, feel, taste and smell, all of which are essential traits to deliver messages and provide evidential proof that their spirit is eternal.

As a columnist for a local newspaper, I am asked many questions from people looking for assurance that their loved ones on the other side are okay and happy, and what is Heaven like. I'm happy to share my knowledge answering some of the most sought-out questions. This book is a compilation of questions, answers, and stories about your loved ones on the other side.

God asked...I listened. My hope is this book brings you peace and comfort when you think about your loved ones on the other side.

Is Heaven Real? (And Is There A "Bad Place"?)

I absolutely do believe in Heaven, and as a medium, I can assure you that it does exist. I know it's easy for me to say since I work with spirit and Heaven every day, and as a medium who does this work for healing purposes, I see a lot of hurt in the world, and certainly circumstances that happen that there are no answers for. I can only tell you what I have been shown and heard from the spirit world.

Early in the beginning of opening up to spirit and using my gifts, spirit would show me in my dream time how beautiful Heaven was. I would come into consciousness and be brought to a beautiful field with flowers and grass, skies so blue, colors so much more vivid and bright. I was shown all the animals walking together in pastures that had no fences, animals that here on earth would be natural enemies but in Heaven were nothing less than loving. One night I sat straight up in bed with amazement as they let me hear the music that is played in Heaven, so much more magical than you could imagine.

It sounds like a fairy tale for sure; I feel I am no more special than anyone else, but I am here to teach the things I see and hear, so others will know with certainty that Heaven does exist. I sometimes now wake to see and hear myself having complete conversations with those I love on the other side – I don't always remember what we were saying, but I do get to see a little of what's taking place. One night I even woke up knowing I was in Heaven having a conversation with my Mom.

Many people assume that if there's a Heaven, there must be that other, darker place. I assure you that there is no fiery existence as has been depicted in books and the movies. I was shown that this "place" exists only as a collection of your own thoughts and state of mind, and when we pass from this state of consciousness, we bring these thoughts with us to the other side.

In Heaven, there are many levels of enlightenment. For example, if you have learned your life lessons and your soul has grown and expanded, you would start at a higher level than someone who has made bad choices for themselves and others. They would start their journey in Heaven at a lower level until more light could be brought to them. Light always takes precedence over dark, just like good always conquers evil.

We are all God's children, and he doesn't want to punish us – he wants us to become the most loving version of ourselves that we can be. Earth is our school room where the lessons are learned. We will never live a life without obstacles to overcome or hard decisions to be made. They are the lessons that we need to go through and learn from, giving our souls the opportunity to learn the unconditional love for others and ourselves.

Your life is all about making choices. Choose wisely for yourself and Earth might seem a little more like Heaven.

What's Heaven Like?

I recently took a poll on my Facebook page asking, "What does Heaven look like?" The responses I got painted a picture of a beautiful, joyful place surrounded by our loved ones.

Once, when I was driving through falling snow, I heard a voice tell me that the snow, swirling around my car and sparkling, looked like what surrounds us as we transition into Heaven. It was peaceful and so very tranquil. People who have had near-death experiences often report that they saw or felt surrounded by a vibrant white, shimmering light – sometimes appearing as a tunnel.

The sky's the limit in Heaven! Whatever your loved one can think of, he or she can energetically manifest in a moment. Whether it's joining you across the world in spirit or participating again in their favorite activity when they were alive, anything's possible for those in Heaven.

Some of my Facebook friends commented that they believe Heaven to be full of nature, completely unspoiled, in heightened, vibrant colors. If their Heaven is a field, it is a field filled with the most fragrant, fully-blossomed flowers and soft, emerald-green grass. If their Heaven is a beach, the sand shimmers like diamonds and the water is the perfect blue.

In all of these visions of Heaven, my Facebook friends included their loved ones who had passed, mentioning their pets and even people who were not related, but close friends and neighbors. They found Heaven to be a place of non-judgment and peace, compassionate and loving.

Our loved ones who had passed from illness or old age are healthy, whole and young again in Heaven. When I do a reading for a client, their loved one may at first appear to me how the client last knew them. The loved one does this purposefully, so the client can easily identify them. As the reading goes on, gradually the loved one will return to the appearance in which they feel best. They may look younger, healthier or simply wearing clothing or accessories that were meaningful to them in life.

Even our pets who have passed on do this! I have seen an elderly dog transform into a puppy and dreamed of an arthritic dog I had bounding joyfully through a grassy field in Heaven. It's so wonderful to see all of God's creations looking and feeling their best again, especially after an illness.

And I can promise you this: when we pass, none of us goes alone. Even if a person passes where there is not another living person beside him, his spiritual team surrounds him. As our vital signs begin to fade, our guardian angels, guides and loved ones who have passed before us step in to accompany us energetically. Even those who are living can feel an energetic shift in the room, to one of peace and acceptance. Our spiritual team leads us through the transition and encourages us thoroughly along the way.

Heaven is right here beside us. It's simply in a dimension invisible to most eyes. And that is why those who have died never leave us. Consciousness is never lost; it is transformed. Thoughts become tangible things, and vice versa. Your reality on Earth can be whatever you choose to manifest. And your Heaven can be just as real.

Hearing The Voice Of God

When I was a little girl, I would hear a man's voice speaking to me, sometimes louder than other times. He seemed to know me well and was always there to comfort me. He would call me "little one." Not knowing who this man's voice belonged to, I associated it with a loving grandfather that had passed when I was two. I thought it must be him trying to guide me. As I got older and still heard the voice, mostly when a big decision had to be made, this voice gave me a sense of knowing who was speaking to me. One day I asked who he was, and pleasantly enough my answer was given: "little one, it's God."

When God talks to me, I hear him outside my head, and I know it's not my or anyone else's thoughts. I feel he has led me this way with a plan all along of me doing the work I do and doing it with him in mind. When I first started giving readings, I left him out of the conversation as it was hard enough to come out of the closet with explaining that I could speak to the dead (they are not that to me). One day, driving down the road, there was that voice, "Little one I need you not to separate me from your work." So, the next reading I gave I said my prayer out loud, as I always start a session with bringing in God, Jesus, and the Angels. I feel totally surrounded by love as I ask your loved ones to talk to me.

I got more confident in my conviction of what I believe and have become more comfortable talking about my conversations with God. God always has a plan - we just are not always aware. I was a nail tech for many years, and one day I asked God, "why did you have me do nails so long?" "I was teaching you to counsel." Well, that was sure true; holding ladies' hands every day listening to the stories of their lives and always trying to be a blessing and wanting them to leave happier than when they came in.

It seemed to make a difference. Anytime we are helping others we are doing God's work. Prayers are heard!

When I was younger and in a nightclub (yes, God was there too!!), my now-husband asked me out on our first date. When I said yes, he held my chin in his fingers just like my dad always did (dad always being my hero), and when I turned around, I heard "you are going to marry him." Talk about predicting the future!! I said "what?" Well, 32 years later we are still happily married. Thank you, God.

He knows I listen. Prayer is like having a conversation with God, but I just walk around talking all the time. He hears. Please know that God wants to talk to all his children and even if you do not hear that voice you might have a feeling, like when you hear people saying God has put in my heart. Different people have different ways of having a relationship with God and the divine. Recently I was letting myself be worried about a situation, and I heard God's voice say, "You do not have Faith." I went to say yes, I do, and then realized if I am worrying, I am not trusting that God knows best. Worrying will not get you where you want to go. Having Faith might just do the trick. I know we are human, and we can tend to get caught up in this Earth life, but if you look deep enough, it's always a lesson that we need to learn. Do your best and follow the Golden rule: Do unto others … and have Faith. Keep talking to God.

Angels Are God's Messengers

Ever since I was a little girl, I had a fascination with God and the Angels. I remember always feeling protected and would stare at the picture my mom had in the house of an angel with the children around her. As I got older, I would buy statues of the angels and would put them in every room in my house and outside in the garden. I started reading countless books on angels and all the different kinds of angels and their strengths, but it wasn't until I started making my connection to the other side stronger that I opened myself up to actually seeing angels.

One night I was reading a book about angels in bed, and I fell asleep with the book next to me. During the night I became conscious of Archangel Michael sitting next to me - so close I could see him staring right back at me. I remembered to ask, "who are you?" He responded, "I am Archangel Michael." On the other side of me was a much bigger-framed angel, and when I looked at him, he said, "I am Archangel Raphael - you are a healer like me." Since that night I have had several visits from Archangel Raphael, especially when I am giving a Reiki session or need healing for myself.

Archangel Michael is with me daily, and I hear him speak very easily and clearly. Doing this work of mediumship and healing, I often need his help with his sword of love and light. I see him almost nightly coming down and taking his sword and scooping the energy left on me by others. When I first started to talk to Michael, I didn't let him stop having a conversation with me for two days. I asked him all sorts of questions: Why can I hear you so well? Why me? All kinds of things until I finally asked, "are you tired of talking to me?" He kindly answered, "no" and said he would be here whenever I need him or to talk. He has for sure kept his word. When I give angel card readings or need advice for someone, he always answers.

I also have heard and seen many other angels, along with fairies, which are the elementals. They are the keepers of the flowers and nature, so if you like to work in your garden call them and ask for a sign. They are smaller and faster than other angels but very pretty and joyful. One night I awoke to a fairy coming towards me, and as she did she came right up close and threw fairy dust at me! Yup, you can't make this stuff up. I told her that was the nicest thing anyone had ever done for me.

Angels love it when you honor them by having statues or pictures of them. It makes them feel wanted. So, if you want an angel to visit you, start by learning as much about them as you can and invite them into your life. They like to be asked, so remember to do so – it's like permitting them to be with you. They can step in and save you if it's a life-or-death situation without you asking. I am sure you have heard of the stories of people surviving death and not knowing how - it was likely the angels stepping in because it wasn't that person's time.

Angels are God's messengers and have never walked on Earth, so if you have a request, state it as simply as possible so they can respond. The most important message I received came one night from two angels, twin brothers Sandelphon and Metatron. These two angels that came to visit me during a meditation told me, "God wants you for something big." I said, "okay," but forgot to ask what. That's okay; I am sure I'll find out.

There is a story of Elijah and Enoch, two twin brothers that did not die, and God took them to Heaven to be by his side, and they became Sandlaphon and Metatron. Metatron is the name Enoch received after his transformation into an angel. Sandalphon is referred to the prophet Elijah, transfigured and elevated to angelic status. I knew nothing about them until the day they visited with me and then did my research. Often when things happen in the spiritual world, I will do research so that I might understand the full story behind them.

Angels Or Spirit Guides?

Who are our angels? People often wonder if a loved one who has passed can become an angel. As much as we may think of our loved ones who have passed as angels, and in our hearts they are, technically they are not, as angels have never walked on Earth.

Guardian Angels are sometimes confused with "spirit guides." A spirit guide is a loving being who has lived on Earth in human form. This person then received specialized training in the afterlife in how to become a spirit guide. Most spirit guides are our deceased loved ones.

Guardian Angels are a unique spiritual energy created by God, to do God's work on Earth and in Heaven. Every one of us is assigned a guardian angel that stays with us from birth throughout our lifetime until we return home to Heaven.

Archangels are the angels who supervise the guardian angels and other angels who are temporarily sent down to Earth to carry out God's work. You can call upon an Archangel whenever you need powerful and immediate assistance. Never think that your problem is too small for an Archangel, or that you are somehow taking away from another person by calling on them. Archangels are not constrained by space or time boundaries on Earth, and their assistance and love energy is endless.

Who are the Archangels? The word "Archangel" comes from the Greek words "arc" and "angel," and basically means "chief angel." There are many Archangels who watch over our guardian angels, and each Archangel has his or her own special area of expertise in dealing with specific human conditions.

One of the Archangels I see and deal with most commonly is Archangel Michael. Michael was the first angel created by God and is the angel of protection, courage, strength, and truth. Michael carries a big sword that he uses to cut through the cords that may be tying us down and to protect us from any negative entities. Call on Michael whenever you are feeling overwhelmed or frightened or just need that extra burst of self-confidence to forge ahead with a project. Michael is invaluable to lightworkers as he assists with protection, space-clearing, and spirit releasement.

You may see feathers floating down as if from Heaven, or hear a soothing whisper in your ear, or even a loud shout to warn you of danger. Many times, it can be a light, comforting touch, or just a sense that someone is with you. There are always signs if you are ready to receive them and know what to look for.

How do I communicate with my angels? The best way to communicate or call upon your angels is for you to simply invite them to come to you. Give them a task – if it is something for your highest and greatest good, they will work with you. We all have God's free will, and the angels will not step in and take control unless it is a life-or-death situation and it is not your time to pass. But if you ask for help, this is like music to their ears. It truly is their pleasure to assist you. When you meditate or otherwise quiet your mind, your angels are better able to communicate with you. That's why so many of us receive our angel messages right before we fall asleep or wake up, or when we are alone, doing something that does not require our minds to be racing in circles. Don't be afraid to ask them for help.

Are You An "Earth Angel"?

Earth Angels, commonly known as lightworkers, are spiritual beings born into physical form to serve humanity. A lightworker or Earth Angel, whichever you prefer, is usually the highly-sensitive men or women that have been sent down here, from Heaven, with a mission to make the world a lighter, happier, more peaceful place to live, while reducing conflict on Earth. Their mission includes helping other souls in the process of ascension, which means rising to a higher level of awareness.

These are the people that seem to be happy all the time, and for no other reason than they just seem to enjoy all the beauty that surrounds them, they are a shining bright light that shines out into the universe making others feel loved while expecting nothing in return. Earth Angels are positive in almost any situation, because of the high vibrational energy that surrounds them. Their mission many times takes precedence over their own wants and needs. Earth Angels are highly-evolved spiritual beings, usually having many of the following qualities: sensitive and gentle, always light-hearted, and full of unconditional love for others, even the tiniest of creatures. Caring to the point of putting others before themselves, putting their own health and happiness last. Seeing only the best in others while trusting to a fault, and often getting their own feelings hurt, sometimes being naïve to situations happening around them. Their goal in life is to be happy and want that for everyone they encounter. Watching harsh stories on the news can be devastating to them, touching their very soul.

Are you an Earth Angel? If you don't like to make others angry and will go to great lengths to keep the peace, or you just can't seem to say no to others, there's a good chance you might be an Earth Angel. Do you feel that you were sent here to make the world a lighter place, always putting others first, and you seem to be on a mission, but you don't know exactly what the mission is? Do you love animals and seem to need their unconditional love for support? Do you have a sense or knowing deep inside that you are a healer, perhaps becoming a nurse or a holistic practitioner? If you see some of these same characteristics in yourself, you might be an Earth Angel.

It's not always easy for the Earth Angel to live on this earth. All the trials and tribulations can take their toll on these loving souls who want only the best for everyone. They feel the energy of the sad or heartbroken people. When this happens, it can leave them feeling like they're not living up to their expectations of themselves. If you think you're an Earth Angel sent here to help the planet to see the light in the darkness, try these tips to help you on your journey of helping others:

Try to eat a diet that is rich in all the colors of the rainbow, bringing you up to a higher vibration. Spend time alone when you need to replenish your energy (it's not selfish). Watch funny movies or read inspirational books, and find a way to restore your soul, and most importantly be yourself because that's what the world needs more of - happy, helpful people that only want what's best for others, while making the world a brighter place to live.

Who's Guiding You?

I can tell you that you have many guides around you at this moment. Before you came down to Earth, you met with your spirit guides to design a blueprint of your life - a blueprint that would enable your soul to have many learning opportunities so that your soul could grow and evolve. Life is our school room for learning, so our guides help us decide which path would be the best for us at this time. You chose the existence that is yours today, and your guides helped with choosing your soul family to be a part of. You are never left alone, as your guides are an important part of your journey. It's so rewarding to meet our team of helpers on the other side.

Meditation and dream time are two of the ways that you can learn to connect with them. Your guides are your spiritual teachers. They give you guidance, knowledge, and wisdom. Angels, family members, ancestors, ascended masters and teachers are just a few who become our guides. Guides help us fulfill the spiritual contract that you made before your trip to Earth this time around. Some guides stay with us throughout our entire life until we are home again, and some are specialty guides that pop in to help with a project or when we need help learning something new.

When I was teaching a dance class many years ago, I would go to bed knowing I had to have the steps down by the next morning, and I would often in my dream time see dancers in Heaven helping me with the steps. If you do not see your guides do not become worried; they are there and are very committed to making sure your life journey is going as planned. They cannot change our free will but are behind the scenes sending us signals that they are around with love and guidance.

It's our job to pay attention to the signs they are sending. Have you ever found a white feather where there is no logical reason for it to appear? Your loved ones, who step into the role of your guide, may have met you or not but are a part of your teaching and guiding team. You may sense them in many ways. Nature plays a big part when they are letting you know they are around. Birds, clouds, rainbows, shooting stars, butterflies and more can all be signs that your loved ones are close by and offering comfort and guidance. It's our job to watch for these signs and pay attention to the world around us every day so we can become one with our guides. When you make the connection to your guides, you will never feel alone on your journey, making life a little easier even if we are on the road less traveled.

Signs From Heaven?

A great deal of what I do deals with not only delivering messages to people from their loved ones on the other side but also telling them about the signs that their loved ones are sending them from Heaven. There are many ways you can receive a message through the signs that are being sent to you; you just have to know what to look for.

My experience shows that dreams – especially vivid, full-color dreams where you have complete conversations with the person who has passed – are the number one way your loved ones communicate with us. Before going to sleep at night, ask to speak with your loved one via your dreams, and ask spirit to allow you to remember that dream when you awaken. Keep a pen and paper by your nightstand, so that as soon as you wake up, you can jot down the dream. The insights can be amazing!

Spirits are pure vibrational energy and can influence another person's thoughts, manipulate electrical currents and sound waves, and create "coincidences" all around us. If dreams don't work for you, spirit will try another method to communicate with you. Some common other signs include:

- Feathers – the sudden appearance of a feather on the sidewalk in front of you or inside a building where no feathers should be could be a sign that a loved one or an angel is watching over you.
- Birds, Butterflies, and Ladybugs – Birds, especially Cardinals, are a very common indicator that someone is sending you a sign or visiting you. Seeing butterflies or ladybugs in unlikely places or times (such as the dead of winter) is also a way that your loved ones can let you know they are near.

- Sound – Hearing music that reminds you of that particular person, especially when you find yourself thinking of them and needing to hear from them, or the sound of someone knocking on your door (but no one is there).
- Electronics – TV's, phones, or even small appliances that turn on/off without logical explanation.
- Pennies or other coins – Finding pennies or coins in places you'd never expect to find them is a very common sign that your loved ones are close by. Look at the date on the coin – it might be a meaningful date for you. If you have just vacuumed and you turn around to see a coin, it was meant for you.
- Numbers in a specific sequence that is meaningful to you, seen repeatedly – as you're thinking of a loved one, check out the time on a digital clock, license plate on the cars near you, or even the numbers as you're doing your bills. You might be pleasantly surprised.
- Smells – The sudden whiff of a specific scent that accompanied a person in his life, such as cigar smoke or the particular perfume that your mom wore, that cannot be explained otherwise. Once, I was sitting in my smoke-free, two-story home, thinking of my grandfather who had passed many years before, and suddenly the whole house smelled like the brand of cigar he used to smoke.

If, in life, that loved one had a special or unique way of communicating their love to you, look for that special sign. For example, before my Dad passed, he would feed a crow that he had become fond of. After his passing, my yard became filled with crows and blackbirds. As I looked out the window and saw this, I said, "Thanks Dad, I know you're okay!"

Orbs From The Spirit World?

Have you ever noticed unexplained balls of light – not reflections from something – but free-floating balls of light or color? These are often referred to as orbs.

Orbs are transparent balls, or globes, or light energy connected to spirits. Orbs are commonly found in photos but can also be seen with the naked eye, particularly around people or in highly energetic areas. These orbs can be a variety of shapes, sizes, and colors.

The colors of orbs can mean different things to different people. Overall, I've seen that the colors of an orb seem to coincide with the energy system in the body called the chakras. Bright, pure orb colors indicate beautiful energy is coming forth. For example, an orb with a red color could indicate a visit from someone who has passed who is sending you strong, protective energy, much like a great big hug for you. White orbs could mean encouraging or inspiring energy, meant to show you that you're on the right path in your life. It all depends on what you see and how it relates to where you are in your life at that moment.

Usually, when I give a reading, the clients' loved ones who are in spirit tell me they have joined them during a celebration or major life events, such as a wedding or family gathering. I find this applies to every one of us. Just as the loved one was with you physically for all the important occasions when they were alive, so they join you again for those events, only this time they are present in spirit. This is why it is so very common to see orbs in wedding photos, graduation pictures, or family reunion snapshots.

Orbs are known as "spirit orbs." Just as orbs are energy, so are we, and so is spirit. Everything that surrounds us is energy and vibrates at an energetic frequency. Actions that raise our vibrational energy and therefore make us more likely to experience orbs, include any spiritual ritual, such as prayer, worship or healing service, such as Reiki. You may also see them while out in nature, which is highly spiritual and places you in a meditative mood, so you are more likely to observe orbs.

Pets, one of my favorite subjects, can easily experience orbs. Cats are particularly adept at seeing orbs. If your dog is wagging his tail or barking at "nothing," he probably sees spirit. Orbs have even been known to play with our pets too. Maybe that's why cats love laser pointers so much.

Some people believe they can see faces inside the orbs. Orbs have been captured with distinctive facial features and even multiple faces in one orb.

Remember, spirits are incredibly creative and persistent in speaking with you. Your loved ones who have passed on will use every energetic tool at their disposal to reach out to you. Dreams, coins, synchronicities and repeated sequences of the same number are some of the methods we've previously covered. Orbs, or light energy, are yet another amazing communication option.

When my father was four, his mother passed away. At night, he would see beautiful flashes and balls of white light above his bed. He found them particularly soothing when he was afraid. Whether these orbs were his mothers' energy or a guardian angel, the result was the same: he felt peaceful and loved. When you see these flashes or orbs yourself, know that someone in Heaven wants to share a sliver of their divine, eternal love with you too.

Children In Heaven?

I've had many people come to me for readings who have lost a child, and they all wonder if I can actually see these children in Heaven and if they are okay. I believe that losing a child is one of the hardest things we can ever go through in life.

I would like to share with you the story of one of the first times I ever saw a child in Heaven. I was at the Omega Institute in Rhinebeck, New York, training at the International Mediumship Week with some of the world's most renowned mediums. James Van Praagh and John Holland were two of my teachers. This was my first experience with training where I had to go and spend a week away anywhere.

Every day, we were shown different ways to bring through spirit. On this particular day, James had us all pair up with another medium (there were 100 of us there). I was matched up with a nice woman who was a little bit older than I and who'd had more training that I at that time. This turned out to be a blessing because "Judy" was a wonderful help.

James asked us to give each other the name, age, and the relationship of someone we wanted to bring through from the other side. Judy looked at me and said, "Ben – he is my nephew and godson, and he is five years old." I looked at Judy with a little trepidation and told her I had never brought through or asked a child to come through to me before. She said, "that is why spirit put you with me."

I did not know how I felt about asking a child in Heaven to join me, but as I closed my eyes for a moment, I saw Ben. I was seeing the smallest boy I had ever seen appear. Ben looked more like three years old and not the five years Judy had given me. She explained that Ben had cancer and had not grown at the same rate as other children his age. Yet, here he appeared before me, happy and healthy-looking despite his small stature.

He came through with vitality and full clarity. I could easily hear him as he was speaking to me. He talked and answered my questions just as any five-year-old would. I could see him standing before me in his little jeans and turtleneck shirt, his dark hair cut with his bangs going straight across his forehead. He was adorable. Ben and I began to have a conversation:

"Ben, do you visit your mom?"

"Oh yes," he exclaimed with joy, "I play all around her feet with my truck."

Ben showed me, in my mind, his mother at the kitchen stove cooking. I told him, "I am here with your Aunt Judy," and with his eyes full of expression he answered, "I like Aunt Judy."

But then his face softened, and he told me, "I miss mommy," which kind of took my breath away.

Trying my best to go on, Judy told me to ask him about his cat.

"Yes, I see my cat. My cat likes to be patted just like this, down the back and up the tail."

Ben showed me the motions, doing this twice in a row. I looked at Judy and gave her his answer.

"Yes," she said, "that is exactly how Ben pats his cat."

"Ben, do you play all the time?"

"I play a lot," he answered with a grin, "but I learn a lot too," showing me that there is school in Heaven.

I could have stayed there talking and interviewing Ben all day, but our time was up, and I had to say goodbye. I thanked Ben for coming to talk to me. The session ended, but before I left him, I told Ben I loved him. He didn't want to leave – he wanted to stay and chat more with me. I finally had to tell him I had to go but encouraged him to go and play with his truck as he had shown me earlier. He did just that with an adorable smile on his face. This new experience made me both sad and happy at the same time, knowing that Ben was very much alive and doing well in Heaven, but still missing his mommy here on Earth, even though he was still very much around her and his favorite cat.

I have had many children come and talk to me since then, even wanting to show me around Heaven. I know in my heart they are cared for and loved by many in the spirit world. They grow at a slower pace there but do grow to help others, even caring for children who come after them and helping them to adjust in making Heaven their new home. Ben visited me a few times after I came home from school that week – I think he knew I was a little sad and that he could cheer me up with his beautiful smile.

If you feel the presence of a child around you, there probably is one. Welcome them with an open heart, because, like Ben, they can hear you. Talk to them, embrace them, and know they are there with you always and that they are okay.

Can You See Babies In Heaven?

Having children in Heaven, I know all too well that feeling of having a hole in your heart. Having had two miscarriages, I often wondered if they were a boy or a girl, and what was the reason they went back home, which is Heaven. Being clairvoyant (seeing), I would get a glimpse of my children in Heaven from time to time. I still always missed them.

Then, amazingly, I saw and heard more from them in different ways. Another medium could see my son peeking out behind a computer and smiling. I was able to link in and see him also. My son told the medium he was sorry that he very much just wanted to be in Heaven longer but loving to be around me as he loved my energy. My son in Heaven looked a lot like my son here on Earth – light skin and red hair and such a nice smile. It did make it easier to bear knowing that he was okay, and it was not my fault, but rather a choice my son had made.

My daughter's soul would also come to visit very often and stand beside my bed and show herself to me. Again, the reddish hair and beautiful eyes of a little girl would stand next to me. My husband, not understanding me, was once awakened in the middle of the night by a little girl, who matched my description perfectly, standing next to the bed. When she realized that he could actually see her, she started to clap her hands out of pure joy, knowing that they had made that connection. My husband even tried to reach out to her, only to have her vision disappear. I believe she was trying to show him what I saw so he would believe also.

I was with a client recently who came in for a reading and asked, "Can I hear from my baby who only lived for a few days?" I took a deep breath, not really sure if a baby could communicate, and sure enough, as soon as she got the question out of her mouth and before I had a chance to answer, here was the face of a young woman. I described the young lady and asked if these traits ran in her family. They did.

I wanted to be a clear channel for the woman to talk, and I heard "that's my mommy!" The number she gave me was the number of years that she had been in Heaven, and her name was Beth. Beth then started to describe in detail the items that her mother had kept since her birth. She showed me a card and described the colors of the beautiful flowers that were on this special card her mom had received when she passed and had kept by her bedside all these years.

Beth wanted her mother to know she, too, was very much involved in the lives of her family, even mentioning her sister. I wasn't sure if a baby that had grown up in Heaven could give me so much evidence, but the evidence did come through loud and clear, and the tears were flowing. Her mom told me that she had waited all this time to be able to communicate with her little girl who had grown into a beautiful young woman on the other side.

This was also a lesson for me because I was not sure myself. But you see, a Soul is a Soul, and there is no time in Heaven – only the unconditional love of family. Please know that if our children are in Heaven, they very much are around you and living life with you, even though it is not in the physical plane. And knowing that our children are okay in Heaven makes the pain of that hole in your heart just a little easier to bear.

Losing A Pet

Losing a beloved pet is just as difficult for some as losing a person from their life. Pets become family members, especially those that give their love and companionship so freely for so many years. I've had several clients come in to see me, wanting to make sure their fur-babies have arrived in Heaven and who they are with. It makes me so happy to see their faces light up with joy when I can describe their pet and tell them that he/she is with Grandma, etc.

Please know that a pet who has gone to Heaven is vibrant and full of youthful energy. They are happy and healthy and having fun with other spirit animals in Heaven, and they are always around you, sending you signs much the same way as humans do. Here are some of the most common signs from your beloved pet:

- You hear their paws padding around the house or running up and down the stairs.
- You hear them purring or panting, or even barking.
- You feel their presence as they curl up on the bed or couch beside you.
- You feel them jump up and leave an impression on the bed or seat beside you.
- You catch a glimpse of them in your peripheral vision.
- You have a happy memory of the two of you together.

Animals are souls as well and have a purpose in this life for each of us. It is their sacred honor to spend their days with us as unconditionally-loving companions. It's no mistake or whim when you bring your pet home with you – it's divinely guided. We are all members of God's kingdom and learn from and love each other. Whatever animal you hold near and dear to your heart is an essential element of both your souls' journeys.

Know that your pets are with you for a reason. Their love is pure and unconditional. Did you know that your pets that pass on could become a spirit guide to you in this life? They can reincarnate as well and go through many lifetimes with you as an ever-faithful companion. They stay by your side in both life and death and will be waiting for you with wagging tails in Heaven, happy to be together again.

Your pets also want to remind you that they know they can never be replaced but would love for you to have a special bond with another pet that needs a loving home. They will be there to help guide you and your new companion through their training in their new home and will be a protective companion to your new addition.

Every night, my Great Dane – Sinbad – who is in spirit now, comes and puts his nose on my nose to say, "Hello from Heaven!" Love never dies.

Totem Animal Guides

If you've been seeing an abundance of a specific type of animal around you, you could be seeing your animal totem or spirit animal.

A totem is defined as a spirit being or sacred object. Spirit animals show up in our lives when we need to learn the lesson that they have to offer. Some Native Americans believe we will be connected to as many as nine different animal totems in our lifetime, all offering different and insightful lessons that we need to learn. Each animal totem is associated with a specific set of meanings and can bring new teachings into our life at different times as we go through our journey here on Earth.

Native American cultures believe that we all have one animal totem that stays by our side through our entire lifetime as our main guardian spirit. Your animal totem has either chosen you or has been chosen for you from the universe to offer you the power of wisdom, respect, and trust. The animal totem that is with you now may change as you grow spiritually or need help with a new lesson. These animal guides are with you in both the physical world as well as the spiritual realm. And while you will have one animal totem as your "forever" guide, you will most likely encounter many others along your journey through life, each providing you with its own important lesson.

I had a client ask me specifically about crows, as she was seeing them everywhere, so I delved into their significance in a little more detail:

*Crows: Crows often appear in groups. Have you ever listened to them cawing? They caw to each other, and each caw has its own meaning. The crow invites us to be our own person and not to follow the crowd. Crow is also an omen of change. They have no sense of time, so they can see the past, present, and future. They ask us to look for the opportunities in life and to bring back the magic that life has to offer. It is said that crows unite both the light and the dark, the inner and the outer, bringing the two together. If you are seeing crows all around you, pay attention to what they represent and see how the lessons they offer can help you on your journey. I hate to admit it, but I actually caw back at them as they do respond (they might be laughing, but that's okay – it keeps my neighbors amused)!

Here are some of the meanings associated with other animals that may be showing up – either in your dream time, or that you are seeing in nature, or those who have been finding you:

BEAR: Instinctive, healing, power guardian, watcher, courage and shows great strength.

BUTTERFLY: Transformation, balance, and grace, the ability to change.

DEER: Compassion, peace, intellectual, gentle, caring, kind and full of grace.

EAGLE: Brave and courageous, shows us to look at the bigger picture and view things with caution but to be confident and to trust your ability. Face your fear of the unknown.

HORSE: Symbolizes loyalty, devotion, friendship, and unconditional love.

These, of course, are just a few, so if you want to learn more about animal guides or who your guides are and who is watching over you, pay attention to the animals that are drawing near to you or that you feel particularly drawn towards. Before you fall asleep tonight, ask for your animal guide to show itself to you. Once you determine what animal is working with you, simply google "animal totems and their meanings." See how this animal resonates with what is happening in your life at this moment in time, and there will be a message. It's all about intention, and the spirit world will work with you.

What's That Smell?

Smelling a fragrance is a sign from your loved one that he or she is close by, and their soul is with you at that exact moment. Smelling is one of the psychic senses called CLAIRALIENCE. Clear smelling. It is less common than the other psychic senses but very much is a sign from Heaven.

When I first moved into my house, I was missing my grandfather, as he had been gone for a long time. I asked one morning to receive a sign from him. That afternoon as I was doing the laundry I started to smell smoke all around me. I ran around thinking there must be a fire, only to find nothing burning. Then I remembered I asked for a sign. The smoke I was smelling was that of my grandfather's pipe he smoked while here on Earth. I made sure to acknowledge his hard work at getting me the sign I asked for.

CLAIRGUSTANCE is the gift of being able to taste something that you have had no contact with. This doesn't happen as often, but it has happened a few times to me. I had a spirit once that really wanted to get a message through that he or she liked pepperoni pizza, something I do not usually eat, but the person on the other side did. It's just another way of giving you signs.

Can Your Loved Ones Or Guides Help You Find Things?

Not only can they help you find things, but they can move things also. Did your dad in Heaven have a sense of humor? Did you think you lost your keys lately? Sometimes, they just like to play around. Keys, small objects – yes, they have that ability, so certainly if you need help finding something call on them for help.

If you need directions and you're on the highway, ask and wait for the answer. How about if you're typing and you need to spell a word you're not sure of? Ask, and see if the answer will come before you let spell-check do the work.

Many people are inspired by the spirit world to write a poem or a song. Many musicians will tell you the lyrics came to them in the night. The spirit world is there to help. Ask, and you shall receive!

Do People Attend Their Own Funerals?

I know they do. With this gift of mediumship, I often take the time at a funeral or wake to acknowledge the person the service is for. Occasionally, I will hear them before seeing them. Lots of times they ask me to tell their loved ones that they are okay. I respectfully do not do that at that time but wait for a later time when it's appropriate.

When a recent family member passed, and we were at the church service, I was amazed when I looked up at the podium to see all her ten brothers and sisters in spirit holding hands together while the service was taking place. It was beautiful to see that our bonds of family hold steady even in the spirit world - standing together hand-in-hand to offer support for their sister as she watched her family and friends saying goodbye to her. Our ties here on Earth strong as in Heaven. A testament of true love and devotion for each other and the unconditional love that never stops, not even in death.

Do Our Loved Ones Hear Our Prayers?

Yes!! Prayers are heard. Our loved ones do their very best to guide us in the direction we want to go in, and we need to do our part. I was told by one of my guides that they may shine a light on a situation but cannot change the circumstance. Keep asking for help in a situation because if they do shine that light, it's sure to be seen. We all have "free will" so if we are asking for something that involves another it might not happen because of the others involved, or it's not in God's timing.

Watching Us From Heaven?

We are watched from Heaven. My client's mom came through from spirit and asked me to tell her daughter that she knew her loneliness and how she missed her mom at night. Her mom showed me herself sitting at the end of the bed, so her daughter would feel the comfort of her presence. I relayed this to my client, and she explained she indeed did feel something on the bed and most times thought it was the cat jumping up, but when she looked there was nothing there.

The next thought her mom sent to me was "tell her I don't watch when she's kissing"! I started to smile and asked my client if that thought had just crossed her mind. The answer was "yes of course"! Her mom assured me she had no interest in that and her daughter had complete privacy when needed. This brings me to the famous question "is my loved one watching me shower?" I can say without a doubt that unless it's a matter of safety with getting in and out of the shower, your loved ones are not spying on you. Protecting and guiding, but never spying.

Looking And Feeling Good In Heaven

When I am conducting a reading, your loved ones come through to me looking like they did here on Earth. They might appear to be younger in age because they have the ability to go back to when they felt and looked their best. They can appear psychically younger and in good health. If your loved one had a leg removed while they were here on Earth, they would show me that they are now whole.

Unless you would not recognize them as their younger self, spirit will appear looking as you would know them. Many 90-year-old soldiers will come through showing me their picture when they were in the service when they were just eighteen. I have the ability to ask them to show me how they looked younger and older. If you would only recognize your Grammy as an older lady that's how she would appear.

That being said, in Heaven, we have no physical bodies. Until recently I didn't quite know what that would look like - until the night before one of my events when spirit showed me they were lining up getting ready for the show the next day. I am sure they were letting me know "no worries - we are ready." I was able to see the pure energy and light, shaped with the outline of our bodies lining up one-by-one. It was amazing and so beautiful to watch!

When I am privy to seeing into Heaven, I do see your loved ones looking very much the same - dressed as they did here, wearing glasses if they did here and enjoying what they loved to do here on Earth. I see them at dinners and gatherings enjoying each other's company. I do tell clients "if you like Dunkin Donuts enjoy your coffee and donut now" because I never see them actually eating or drinking. They don't physically need to do that anymore. Someone coming through that had a sweet tooth while here on Earth might show me a birthday cake if a celebration of a birthday is near, telling me to tell them to "have a piece for me."

Visit The Cemetery If It Makes You Feel Good

Spirit often tells me "Please tell my loved one" I see them planting flowers, visiting the cemetery, cleaning up around the stone. They very much do appreciate the thought and concern you have for them. It shows you honor them, and they are grateful.

They are not in the cemetery (except when you're there), but they do try to leave you a sign to let you know they are close by. I have been visiting my parents' grave and taking care of the flowers, and every time I go, I hear (not see) a cardinal talking up a storm to me. I always smile and say hello to my parents and thank them for their sign. Last time I drove home, and as I was pulling into my driveway, a cardinal flew right past the front of my car. I let them know that was pretty fancy!

Seeing "Spirit" All The Time?

Many people have asked me this question "Can you see people all the time?" – Like if I'm in the grocery store, do I see spirits following around the shoppers that are there? If I did, I'd never get my own shopping done!

Really though, a trained medium also knows how and when to tune in to be able to see and hear spirit. The spirit world wants us to live our lives on Earth as normally as possible, so we learn how to tune in and how to tune out. The people that come up to me and say they see or hear spirit all the time are the ones who have not learned to control or work with spirit on that level.

That's not to say spirits don't pop in on me sometimes when I least expect it – like the time I was shopping in a bookstore that had old World War II model planes hanging from the ceilings. As I looked up at them, I saw a soldier who informed me that he had indeed flown a few of them. I thanked him for his service and kept shopping.

How Many Messages Can You Deliver In A Day? (And Does It Take A Lot Out Of You To Do So?)

Different mediums would give you different answers to this question. For me, I always want my messages to be clear and spot-on, so I limit the hours I am working with spirit each day.

Giving a message from your loved ones is all energy work, and it can affect the nervous system. We are all energy, and for me to communicate with the Divine, I need to raise my vibration while they need to lower theirs, so the two worlds can meet.

Doing this work is like anything else – we need to take care of ourselves. Getting enough sleep and exercise, and a diet that consists of healthy foods helps make us a strong conduit for being a strong communicator.

Do Angels Have Wings?

I see angels with wings, but also with beautiful faces, and each having different jobs to do. I have seen angels gently lay their wings across bodies of people requesting healings, and I have also felt them wrap their wings around someone who needs comforting.

If you want to see, hear or feel angels, ask them to assist you. Angels like to be asked so as not to go against your own free will. If you want to be closer to the angels, invite them into your home. Adding statues or reading a book about them seems to bring them near.

I have a statue or night light of angels in every room, welcoming them in.

Who Will I Hear From In Spirit?

Many people have come to me for readings wanting to hear from one particular person, and sometimes that person may not be ready to come through yet. I always say it's not "spirit-on-demand." If we do request for someone special to come through, they will eventually. It does take time for our loved one to have enough energy to come through. Much as I have had the training to speak to them, they need time to learn to speak with us.

Some spirits are better at communicating than others. Don't be discouraged if at first a loved one who has been in spirit for a longer period comes through first and then brings forth the person you wanted to speak to. They do that. It's like showing them the ropes.

If your person does not come through, they just might need a little longer to build up that energy. Usually, the first person to come through for you will have the strongest messages that you need to hear at that time of your life.

Remember, the spirit world and your loved ones only want the very best for you.

Can Someone Who's Been Gone A Long Time Still Come Through?

Absolutely! One of my favorite groups of people to talk to in heaven is grammies! They always seem so wise and hard-working, full of love, and they hold lots of cherished memories.

It doesn't matter how long someone has been gone – they are your soul family and are very much watching over you and your journey here on Earth while sending you signs to give you guidance on this bumpy road we call life. They cannot change a situation, but they can shine a light over it, making it a bit easier to go through.

Why Haven't I Heard From My Loved One? (Tips For Communicating With Your Loved One)

One of the questions I get asked a lot is "why haven't I heard from my loved one?" Sometimes when we are missing someone we've lost, the grief we are feeling can be overwhelming, and in the depths of it, can block us from seeing the signs that a loved one sends to us. This is especially true if we were the person who was the closest to the one who has passed, and we are just too entrenched in the rawness of our grief to see and feel the messages from Heaven.

It's easy to miss the signs they are sending, though they are there. Take comfort in the signs that your friends and family members receive from your loved ones. They are purposely sent to them because your loved ones know they can receive and communicate them to you when you are unable to.

Be open to receiving. Many times during a reading, loved ones in Heaven will tell me how they are trying to reach out and start the communication, or ways that they are coming through to give you a sign, and when I tell clients what to look for, many have already been seeing the signs and not understanding that they were from spirit. Sometimes signs can seem like a coincidence.

Pay attention to what's happening around you. Are the lights flashing in the room you're in, or are the dogs barking or wagging their tails back and forth for no apparent reason or explanation? Animals often see spirit and can see who is coming to visit with you.

Notice what your children are saying or doing. If you see your children having a conversation with someone who's not there, it's more than likely that their grandparents are stopping in and keeping a helpful eye on them. Grandparents are very invested in knowing their grandchildren, even if they were not born before their passing.

Don't be stressed. Try to give your loved ones in Heaven the time they need to come through. In the meantime, try to hold them close in your heart and acknowledge their lives by speaking about them often and honoring the lives they lived while here on Earth. They love it when their memory is kept alive! And when the messages start to flow, be sure to let them know you are receiving them, so it truly is a conversation from Heaven. Let the conversation from Heaven truly be a blessing. It's a beautiful reminder that love is eternal and that we are surrounded by those we love, constantly, whether here or in Heaven.

Grief, Dying, And Your Higher Self

Everyone grieves differently, some openly showing their feelings and emotions, while others hold them inside and hope that they become easier and less painful with time. As a spiritualist, we believe in the continuance of life after death, and as a medium, we offer proof that our souls continue to thrive and grow, just not in the same physical way as we were accustomed to here on Earth. We leave our ailments and sickness behind, much like taking off a winter coat, but our souls continue to keep the same personality and little quirks that we have loved about that person while they were here with us.

Loved ones not only continue to stay around us - they are very much invested in our lives – but they are always guiding and watching their families grow and thrive here on Earth. They cannot change our paths, but very much are involved in helping us make the right decisions for ourselves while shining a bright light on situations that need our attention.

Have you ever been awakened in the middle of the night with a great idea that you thought was your own? That thought or idea might have been given to you from your loved one, a guide, or even your higher self. Yes!! - Your higher self - you do have one. It's that little voice that asks you to always do the right thing, always looking out for your highest and greatest good. We all have one - it's our spiritual side within each one of us. Some of us are more attuned to listening to that little voice inside than others.

Our higher self is the very best of us and works hand-in-hand with spirit. It's that voice in your head that directs you to give someone a chance instead of filling yourself with doubt and dark thoughts about them. Your higher being is always looking for the good in others and pointing out their attributes, not clinging to their faults or failures. When we are grieving or hurt we can sometimes let those emotions rule our head and hearts, and we just need to look deep inside to find our higher selves within our souls.

Grief or hurt feelings can sometimes bring out the part of us called the EGO (Edging God Out). I am sure you can remember a time or two when your own ego has reared its ugly head. When we let our emotions rule our lives without stopping to see the good or (GOD) in everyone, our egos can do damage, sometimes damage that cannot be erased. Our ego tries to keep us tied to our earthly emotions instead of living with faith and compassion for others and seeing the good in all living creatures. I call this the "what ifs." What if we had a better job? Marriage? More money? What if we had what our neighbors had? We can get lost in these emotions and feelings. Thankfully, our higher self is there to raise us up.

There is always going to be someone that has less than you and others who have more. It's learning to be happy with what you have that makes the difference between enjoying a happy life or a life filled with pain and envy.

Next time your emotions start to get the best of you, take a moment and ask yourself this simple question: Is this my higher self or my EGO doing the talking? Yes, grief and hurt feelings can seem too hard to conquer, but when it does, give it up to your higher self and God. Most importantly, if you are in the grieving process, give yourself time to heal and take all the time you need. A broken heart can seem like forever. Try to see the big picture - one that is filled with love and joy and most importantly Peace.

Holding On To Guilt?

It's not easy to move forward when you are holding on to the feeling of guilt because you had to make some hard, final decisions at the end of a loved one's life. Unfortunately, guilt is a natural and common component of grief. We somehow feel that we failed in our duties and obligations, or that we've done something wrong.

We can feel that we didn't do enough or could have changed the outcome in some way. It's only human to look at what you did or did not do and start to dwell on the "what-ifs" and "if onlys." It's best to know in your heart that you did your best and your loved one in Heaven does not want you to feel anything but love. They know you would only have done what was best for them. They are always by your side, watching out for you. They want you to let go of any regrets or guilt and to go on living a happy and fulfilling life with your loved one still in your heart.

It's important to try to remember all the good things you have done in your relationship with your loved one and all the loving care you shared. All the memories of what you did together that brought you joy, laughter, and excitement are the important things to hold onto and keep close.

Truly your loved ones want you to be happy. Try to picture a situation where if the tables were turned you surely would want nothing more than for your loved one to go on and for you to bring them vicariously with you on your journey.

Everyone grieves in his or her own way and own time. Take the time you need to heal. Do good deeds in your loved one's honor. Take time for yourself, cry when you need to, be kind and compassionate with yourself, and sooner than later only the happy memories will remain.

If an unhappy thought does come into your head, there's a great trick to getting the bad thought out and the good in. When an unhappy thought comes to you, take a moment to say, "clear, clear, clear" three times, and replace the unhappy thought with something that brings a smile to your lips. Soon only the happy thoughts will reside.

Could My Mom Hear Me? (Parents With Alzheimer's)

I often have clients that come in wondering if their parents who had Alzheimer's could understand or hear the words that were spoken to them. I can assure you that even though it didn't seem that they could hear in the physical world, their soul heard every word that was spoken or whispered in their ear. Your mom knows the love and concern that you had for her and the love that you hold in your heart.

Our bodies may not last forever, but our soul is eternal and carries all the information within ourselves. Our soul has had many life journeys and will continue until the day we decide we have learned all the lessons we have wanted to learn, as our soul continues to expand and learn from each lifetime here on Earth. We come down to Earth with our soul family - this family was formed before our journey began. You picked your mom and dad and the rest of your family (yes, even your siblings) for the lessons and things your soul wanted to learn in this lifetime. Your siblings and soul family can be here to teach you some of those toughest lessons. The Earth is our school room, a place to learn, and Heaven is our home. It's hard to think that we picked certain lessons to learn while here this time on Earth. Making tough decisions might have been something that you chose to learn so your soul would recognize certain aspects of feelings and emotions.

As we learn our lessons that we chose here, our hearts and souls open up to greater knowledge and love. We understand what it feels like to have had to make hard decisions that affect others. If we look at the circumstances that happen to us in our everyday lives, we start to realize there is a lesson in almost every choice or situation that is happening to us. As we look deep into our trials and tribulations, we can try and decipher what lessons are hidden in the problems that we are experiencing. Many people go through life trying to learn the same lessons, making the same mistakes in their life over and over again until one day a light bulb goes off and they see the lesson for what it is. This is when they can see the lesson and learn from it. Every lesson is not a punishment, but a way for our soul to keep on growing.

I often tell my clients if there were no trials and tribulations in our lives and everything was always happy and carefree, that our souls would not be able to learn the valuable lessons that we all came down here to learn. Our hearts and souls open up and expand as we learn empathy and how to feel compassion and sympathy for others. It makes us better people when we know how others are feeling and we feel for them. We all are learning these lessons. When we realize what the lessons are we can say thank you, I understand, handle it with grace, and then ask that the lesson is taken away.

When we get to Heaven is when we find out in our life review how we did with the lessons that we chose. Not to judge, but to see where we handled things and learned from them, or how we could have done better. I tell clients to learn your lesson this time around, so our souls can grow, and we don't have to bring the same lesson with us next time we come back to the Earth plane.

I am not immune to these lessons myself, so I know how hard it is to have a parent that has Alzheimer's and has to be in a care facility. I now understand the lesson of having no control over certain situations and having to surrender to that feeling. I know why I had to learn that lesson as I always want to be in control. There is a deep-hearted feeling when you seem to have no control over what is happening in your life and the feelings that come with it - I now understand this.

Know in your heart that you did the very best with your mom in the situation that you were given. Our parents only feel the love that we have for them, and their souls know the lessons that had to be learned. Heaven is our home, and their souls are now free from any disability and illnesses that they had while here on Earth. I used to tell my dad, "Dad you get to have all your horses back when you get to Heaven," and he would say "I'll have a herd" (he was brought up having horses). I see him now in Heaven, and when he shows up, he brings his horses with him. They are now watching out for us and hear your thoughts and prayers so have no regrets – it's only the love that matters.

Can You Be Angry At Someone In Heaven?

I give a lot of readings where a child is angry at a parent. It's a tough one because they are not physically here to talk things over with. Children can be holding onto the thought "I wish I could do it all over again - I would speak up this time or take a stand about something I didn't believe in." They have a regret; "I should have, could have, done something different or spoken up about the injustice that was placed with me." They feel they could have been stronger and spoken their truth when they had the chance. It's okay to feel this way, but it's good to try and let go of these pent-up feelings.

Some children can be resentful for having lived through the divorce of their parents, while others feel abandoned by a mother or father who had left them, either mentally or physically. The reasons can go on and on. It's okay to know that your feelings are your feelings and you have every right to them.

What you do need to know is that if you suppress those feelings deep inside of you where you cannot see them on occasion, they will pop back out at you. It's like looking at the face of a clock. If there's a problem at two o'clock and it doesn't get fixed the hand will keep going around and around again, but it always will end up back at two. If the problem doesn't find a way to resolve itself and you haven't fixed it, then it will be hanging around until the next time. In other words, we need to come to peace with troubles or resentment, or they are going to stick around.

Now that we know our feelings are not going to be dismissed, we need to fix them so that we can flush them out of our systems. How do we do that when the person we are mad at is no longer here? One way is to have a conversation with the person in Heaven that you have the grievance with. You say, "well that's not so easy," but isn't it? Our loved ones are always with us whether we are mad at them or not. They know your thoughts! Go to a medium that you trust to have that conversation with you. FROM SPIRIT, THROUGH SPIRIT, TO SPIRIT. You can have an actual conversation with a medium or take it upon yourself to start the conversation in your own space.

Sit in a quiet area, a place where you can meditate and be alone with your thoughts. Take a piece of paper and write down your regrets or grievances and be honest with yourself. Sit and think about what you would say if they were here now. Believe me, they can hear you. Try to forgive them as it helps not only them but you also. Please remember, after they passed they had a life review to see where they could have done better with you, so go easy on them because they have regrets also. In Heaven, only the love shines through for us.

Your loved one was always full of love for you here and wanted to keep you from harm's way, even if their way of showing it wasn't what you wanted it to be. Take control of your life now that he/she no longer has any influence on you and live life to its fullest. Your life now is yours to do with exactly as you would like. Let go of the past. Now is your time.

Do Parents In Heaven Choose Sides?

Family conflict is a very common and very trying situation for many families. Battle lines are often drawn and parents and siblings often "take sides" with one or another. Many people have wondered if these divisions still occur in Heaven – do parents still take sides with children who are not getting along?

We all know that these difficult relationships with our siblings can serve to teach us some very hard lessons, and it's not so easy to go through the process of finding peace. Please know that no family is perfect, and if we try to achieve perfection or our idea of what a family is supposed to look or act like, we might be greatly disappointed. Every family can have drama, but it is up to us how we respond to it. We have no control over how others react, only our own response.

Whenever I have been giving a reading and had a client ask, "what does my mother think of how my sister or brother has been treating me," I pause because I know what they want to hear. We all want to hear that our siblings have made bad choices or decisions, that we are in the right and want our parents support, and for them to stick up for us on the other side. I always ask and listen to what a mom or dad has to say, but it rarely sounds close to what we expect.

You see, Heaven is all about unconditional love, and there is no judgment. That doesn't mean a parent wants to see their child in harm's way, but when it comes to pointing fingers, they just don't do it. They have a better view of a situation then we do, and they look into the soul of their child here on Earth to see why this sort of behavior is happening. We don't always know why our siblings are striking out at us or trying to hurt our feelings, but by looking at that person as a soul instead of just a sibling, we sometimes are better able to see where they are coming from.

Every parent here or in Heaven wants their children to get along and love each other. It's the best gift you can give your parents. Nothing makes them happier than seeing their children showing love for each other. There are lots of reasons why grown children can be at odds with each other. Feelings of jealousy or rivalry are just a couple. But what seems most important to parents is that their children can find a way to be at peace with one another. When parents are gone, it's the children that are left with the task of keeping the family held closely together. If the parent was the glue that held the family together the family can start to unravel.

What can you do to keep your family close? Try to find peace, even if it means you being the peacemaker. Try not to pass judgment on your siblings or their children. Remember, everyone is on their own journey here and might not always meet the expectations that you have for them. Try to make your siblings see that they are important to you, sharing your struggles and accomplishments with them.

Try to stay connected, even if it's just a phone call. If there's a problem, try to get to the root of it as soon as possible by being honest and asking, "why are you behaving this way to me?" Work with them to find a solution. Where there's a problem there usually is a solution if you look deep inside your heart. If you have created wounds, try to heal them. Healing can take time; all you can do is your best. Remember that your siblings have been with you throughout your lifetime - it would be sad to let differences get in the way.

Soul Contracts

Some families always seem to have so much drama going on – is it just a clash of strong personalities, or is there a bigger, more spiritual cause? Often, there are many life lessons that need to be worked out within these family dynamics, which brings me to the subject of Soul Contracts.

Families, particularly parents and their children, are some of our most tangible soul contracts. Before we were born into our current lifetime here on Earth, we agreed with God, our guides, and those who incarnated along with us, to take on specific learning tasks. Many times, these are centered on themes like forgiveness, honoring boundaries, loyalty, or understanding other major life lessons. These major life lessons are called soul contracts.

Soul contracts are what each of us has agreed to grapple with throughout our lives. The irony is that often our soul contract appears to hinder or block us, when it is, in fact, serving us. The hardest lessons are our best teachers, and we can only learn from experience.

Our souls place people, experiences and events in our lives to guide us in our path to recognize and resolve our soul contracts so that we may remember our own power – our "wow" moment.

If we don't understand it the first few times, the lesson will emerge as a pattern and continue until we do. Once we recognize it and learn from it, we can release the pattern and grow.

For instance, a person whose parent left the family while he or she was young, and then as an adult either pushes people away or has trouble maintaining a stable relationship, has the soul contract of abandonment. Once that person arrives at this realization and does the necessary inner work to resolve those feelings, he or she grows in leaps and bounds spiritually. The soul contract is fulfilled, and the negative pattern slips away.

Soul contracts can appear in a brief relationship or within a 50-year marriage. Sometimes it may even take us a series of lifetimes to learn one specific lesson. Regardless, whenever we encounter these major life themes, we instinctively realize their importance. These are life's hardest lessons, but they are also the most significant.

One thing that is not predetermined by your soul contract is your free will. Even though your basic pathway has been set, your life is full of choices that you do have control over. No one can take that away from you. And all choices will eventually lead to self-knowing – either in this lifetime or the next. Some pathways are simply bumpier or more meandering than another.

Sometimes we can get off that path that we have set for ourselves. You'll know it when you feel "lost," confused, or even physically sick. Because we are always surrounded by our spiritual team, you'll find that you are presented with multiple opportunities to get back on track. Once you are on the chosen path, you'll feel like yourself again – confident you're heading in the right direction.

I know it's difficult to see family situations that aren't ideal, but these challenges have been purposely pre-arranged by you and God to help your self-growth. Try to see everything out of the unconditional love that God has for you. We know He'd only give you what you can handle, so rise to the occasion and accept the challenge.

Think of how empowering it would be, and the incredible relief you'd feel, to finally release the problem that's been plaguing your family. Reflect on the situation and ask yourself "what is the life lesson I need to learn here"? Listen quietly for the answer – seek and you will find. You'll be so happy you did.

Grudges In Heaven?

Can a person who passed have a negative effect on someone here if they passed holding onto a grudge, or worse? Can they have a negative effect on the living?

That's a very good question - I bet a lot of people think about this question but never seem to ask about it. I myself had wondered about this very same question before I became more familiar with how Heaven works. Say you had a relationship that didn't end too well, or maybe a divorced spouse that you had not come to any reconciliation with, and they were still holding onto jealousy, anger or even had hate in their heart? How would that affect you here? We hope that this is not the scenario, but this is Earth, and we are here to learn lessons, so our soul can become complete. What if someone didn't learn the lesson of forgiveness before they passed? I can tell you with confidence that I have never heard a spirit say, "I'm still angry."

When we pass, we go through this beautiful transition to a higher plane, and we have a life review. That's where we see and feel everything that we have done to ourselves and others on our journey here. Every time we said hurtful things or did something out of meanness, our review shows us how we made the other person feel. Not so that we are judged, but rather only to see how we have could have handled the situation differently. We now get to see the bigger picture and why some things happened the way they did. They were all lessons.

When we enter the Heavenly realm, all those heavy bad emotions are taken away. No more are we holding onto 'why did this, or that happen to me' or 'why was I treated this way.' Those emotions are no longer held onto - almost like a big weight being lifted off of our shoulders. We feel relief. I do know that spirits tell me they do have regrets for their wrong-doings and very much want to tell that person or family member "hey,

I'm so sorry for my actions or my part in the relationship that went bad. I now know, I'm sorry, and I wish for forgiveness". Unconditional love is all you're going to receive from Heaven because that is what Heaven is all about - the unconditional love for yourself and others.

Do not have the fear that someone who has passed can do any harm to you here on Earth because that just won't happen. If you have had someone who has passed, and you weren't on good terms with them while they were here, be the bigger person and send them love and light up to Heaven. It not only releases heavy emotions that you are carrying in your heart but also helps their soul to feel the forgiveness and continue to grow. You don't need to condone something bad that someone has done to you or holding a grudge against you, but you do need to release the emotion and let it go for your own sake and well-being. Send a prayer up to Heaven that you forgive them and move on, feeling confident that only Love comes from Heaven.

Can One Make Peace With Those Who Have Died?

You've had a complicated relationship with a relative who was not a perfect person in life. In fact, when she died, you'd been estranged for many years. If Heaven isn't a place where grudges exist, what happens when the person passes with unresolved relationship issues? Is it safe to assume that the other person is all set and forgives (and is forgiven for) the toxic relationship?

This situation comes up all the time. First of all, no one on Earth is perfect: this is our schoolroom, and we are here to learn and grow from our mistakes. If we were all perfect, we wouldn't be on Earth in the first place!

Because no one is perfect, naturally, when we die, many of us leave with unfinished business. When we go to Heaven, we are given a life review, where we are shown the major choices we made during life. We see it all: the good we have done, where we have lifted others and made the world a better place, and also the decisions that were hurtful and failed others. During this review, we actually feel what it felt like for someone when we hurt them. We are given this life review not to be judged, but so that we can learn from our lives. Remember, Earth is our schoolroom and life is our education.

When recalling a situation with someone with whom you've had a difficult relationship, ask yourself and ask God "what lesson do I need to learn from this"? By reframing your perspective in this way, the life lesson will become clear. Sometimes you'll learn patience or to be humble. Sometimes you'll learn acceptance. And sometimes you'll learn the value of self-care and setting boundaries. Once that lesson is realized, you'll find the situation stops happening. The life lesson has been learned, and you can move on.

I was taught by a famous medium that we must do our best to leave for Heaven without any regrets. If we extend our hand for forgiveness and it is not accepted, then it is no longer our baggage. It is that of the person that did not accept our apology. Always try to be the bigger person – always try to make or accept an apology.

Yes, you can make amends in the afterlife! It is incredibly healing for all involved. I have seen so many people leave a reading with me with a new light in their hearts, unburdened at last because they were able to say or hear "I'm sorry." I have also seen those in Heaven finally be able to communicate what is in their heart to their loved ones here on Earth. They heal, too, and once they convey their message, their soul is able to move on from the situation and continue to grow.

Heaven is all about unconditional love, but people are people on Earth as in Heaven. So, try to make amends for mistakes or hurt feelings, because you do not want to be here or in Heaven with regrets.

Pain In Heaven?

I can assure you there is no pain in Heaven. Once you leave your body, you are no longer in any pain. Unfortunately for us, we tend to remember how our loved ones died, rather than the life they lived. Try to hold onto the memories of your loved ones in their younger years when they had no aches or pain and were in perfect health. This is usually how they appear to me unless you would only recognize them in their later years.

Just as an example - my brother, who had his leg amputated in the physical world, once in Heaven came to me through a dream, showing me himself with a cowboy hat and he was dancing!! He was restored to perfect health and wanted me to see this myself. It's now a perfect memory for me. We are not our bodies; we are souls living in a body having a physical experience.

If There's Pain, There's A Healing

In addition to the heartbreak that comes with losing someone close to us, we can often feel physical pain, complicating our ability to recover or receive messages from our loved ones.

Pain can manifest in many ways. Both emotional and physical pain are messages from our body that we need to stop and pay attention. While emotional pain can let us know that something in our psyche needs some attention, focusing in on our inner awareness, physical pain can provide us with proof that we need to dig deeper and see where all this pain is manifesting from, getting to the root of the problem and hence easing the pain. Both physical and emotional pain can wreak havoc on our lives if not dealt with and are swept under the rug.

When someone passes our heart can feel like it's breaking. But other symptoms may also occur. We need to uncover the message of our pain. Our bodies know how to send signs to us that something is going on and needs our undivided attention. With a broken heart over the loss of someone or something, we need to ask ourselves if this is the normal grieving process and will we just need some time to adjust to our new normal? Or in cases where the pain is lingering or taking a toll on your life's day-to-day activities will we need to do something more to get through it. If it's the latter, don't be ashamed to ask for help. Friends and relatives usually have a good listening ear, and a counselor would also be a good choice.

Physical pain can manifest in all different forms in our body. We are made up of an energy system. The Chakra system (our energy centers) runs from the top of your head to the tip of your spine. These centers are all vibrating and spinning at different rates of speed and have a different color associated with each. The Chakra centers are where energy comes into and goes out of our bodies. These centers can become slower or not running at full capacity, and a dis-ease can take place. Sometimes it's a good idea to have a professional Reiki practitioner appointment with someone that knows how to clear those chakras and put your body back into balance. A Reiki appointment can do no harm, and the energy will go to where it is needed most psychically, mentally and emotionally. Remember to always consult with your own doctor with any pain you might be having.

If we listen to our pain, we will know how to evaluate it and come up with the solution that is right for us. The next time you feel a pain try listening to your own intuition about how to relieve it. The message, in the end, is not about the pain but the healing.

Give Your Home A Spiritual Cleaning

Sometimes cleaning our homes and clearing our psychic energies are one and the same. When we live in a cluttered, dark or dirty environment, we can become depressed, absorbed in our problems and isolated.

When we donate or sell items that we no longer use and that are only cluttering our space and our minds, we release that extra energy – which is really a burden – and find it liberating. Opening windows to let the sun and the sounds of nature in is also psychically cleansing. We are literally letting the light in! And sounds from nature – sometimes referred to in metaphysical circles as a sound bath – is another way of purifying and aligning the energies of a person or place.

Because we are of nature, we can look to the natural world for ways to ready ourselves for the new season. In the spring, as you know, tender plant buds push through the soil to bloom, and animals shed their excess fur to lighten their coat. Shed your "coat" too – clean the dust off both your home and your psychic environments this season. Release anything that does not serve you. Forgive past hurts and misunderstandings so that you, too, can push through and bloom in the light.

Now that you know the reasoning behind a spring cleaning, I'll share the exact steps I personally use to clear my own home each spring. You'll only need a few tools: sage (either loose or bundled as a smudging stick), a wide, flat shell to use as a bowl (or a bowl that can contain burning embers), a feather, and matches. That's it! Once you've gathered these items, you're all set to go.

You can get the items in any metaphysical store; even a health-food store should have them. Even better, you can find the shell yourself for free, on a beach, and the feather on a nature walk. We will use these tools in a process called smudging – a cleansing and healing ritual that has been around for thousands of years and comes from Native American culture. The act of burning the sage and fanning the smoke around the room with a feather removes the old and brings in the new. And with it comes healing on a spiritual, physical and emotional level. The smoke is what does all the work, bringing with it all that needs to be cleared as it ascends to the Heavens.

So, let's begin! Standing with your smudging stick or your loose sage in the shell, light the end(s) with a match and let it burn for a few seconds before gently blowing the fire out. The resulting smoke is what you want to work with. First, hold the shell or bowl carefully above your head and say a prayer of intent to remove any energy that is clinging to you. You may call in your ancestors, angels, guides and/or great spirit to ask for their help with this ritual. They hear you and are glad to help. Use the feather to gently push the smoke in your direction. Next, you will want to continue in this way, working down the length of your trunk, legs, and arms. Visualize the negative and the old, unwanted energy going down into Mother Earth, where she will send it back up, transformed once again.

When you have reached your feet, bring the shell back up to the top of your head. Fan the smoke to the back of you all the way down. Waft the smoke all around you, with you in the center. Give thanks to all. When you have finished, step away and breathe in love, courage, and a new feeling of strength.

Now you are clear and purified, and you're ready to clear a room or a home! Ensure that your sage is still letting off smoke and move into the middle of the room to begin. Call in all the positive energies available to you. Waft the smoke to the four corners of the room, top to bottom, moving around the room in a clockwise manner facing the North, South, East, and West.

Then, back out of the room through the doorway, and "seal" up the doorway to the room with smoke. Let the smoke sit in the room collecting all the old energy for five minutes. Lastly, open a window or a door to let in fresh air and allow the remaining smoke to leave. Give thanks for all who guide and protect you.

Wow! Give this a try and feel the difference in the atmosphere in your space and the lightness in your body!

Your Divine Purpose?

When we chose to come here this time to have an Earth experience, we chose a blueprint to follow. We always choose a job or career that will fulfill our destiny and open ourselves up for soul growth. If the job you are in now does not feel rewarding to you any longer, it may be time to ask yourself what would make you happy.

The universe always wants us to be enjoying our time here on Earth, so when they make things difficult, it usually means it's time to move forward. If your job were still satisfying to you, you wouldn't have these feelings of "is there any more than this?" It might be time to ask yourself "what would bring me joy and still make the money I need to pay my bills?" Dig in deep and ask yourself what you believe you are supposed to be doing for work. Where do your interests lie? What makes your heart fill with excitement when you think of doing this job all day long or even part-time? Think about what comes naturally to you. Are you good with children? Animals? Writing? Then think of how you could use your talents to bring in the money you need while at the same time fulfilling your soul purpose.

Your soul purpose usually involves helping others in some way. We are all born with different talents - it's a given. Whether we choose to grow these talents and use them to make the world a better place is up to us. It comes with our "free will" that no one can take away. Our talents can come with challenges that we may need to overcome - the person that has a beautiful voice but is too scared to stand in front of an audience, or the person that feels everyone is better than them at their trade. When we overcome our hang-ups and insecurities is when our true self can shine. It might take some work if you lack self-confidence, but it sure will be worth it in the end to see the results of your hard work.

Going out of your comfort zone to try new things is not easy, and that's when you want to ask for help. If it was meant to be and you're putting in the work, it will happen. Our jobs take up a lot of our time here on Earth, so make sure you are satisfied with what you are doing and not just playing it safe. Life is for having FAITH and taking chances. I am not saying quit your job and wait for a miracle, but I am saying start to take actions towards your goal. When you put your energy into making things happen, you will start to manifest what you truly desire. If you need to start small by taking classes or finding a mentor, start there. Life should be about enjoying our time here and at the same time helping others along the way.

Writing Your Obituary?
(How Do You See Your Life?)

In 10th grade my high-school history teacher had us sit and write our obituary. We were so young and had not really started to live life. Why would he ask us to do this you say? He wanted to show us how our life could look in the end. How do you want others to see you when you're ready to leave this earth? I am sure we all looked a little perplexed staring up at him. He told us many great people in history have done amazing things and have amazing stories of how they accomplished their goals in their lifetime. My teacher wanted us to envision what we could do with the time we had here. He wasn't trying to scare us as much as he wanted us to take a good long look into the future. To truly see what we could manifest while having the best life possible for ourselves while making the difference in someone else's life or lives. To truly live a life worth living.

We sat in class and tried to write the best story of how our lives would unfold. I remember very clearly envisioning a happy marriage and children and having a happy future. Besides that, I am not sure what I wrote down, but I do know it stuck with me this whole time. In fact, every time I have accomplished a new goal or gone to places I've always wanted to go I imagine it written down in my obituary. Sounds kind of eerie you say but really, it's about living a fulfilled life and being proud of the life you are living.

What do you want others to remember about you? Ask this question as you move forward. What do you want to be remembered for? I have had a happy marriage and family which I am so grateful for, something I never take for granted. Think of your obituary as a vision board. What is your calling? How do you want to fulfill your souls' calling? Is work just a paycheck to you or is your work helping others in some way? Are you happy as you look back at where you've been and how far you got? Are your goals coming to fruition or have you let them sit on the sideline waiting for someone to step in and take action?

This is your time to write your obituary. If you don't like that idea sit and write down your life's plan you have for yourself. We only have so much time here; with a little planning, it can be filled with love, compassion, and fulfilled dreams. Go big, dream big, what can it hurt?

When you write down what you truly desire it gives the universe permission to step in and help with our plans. How do you want to be remembered? More importantly, what do you want for your life?

Are You An Empath?

How can you tell if you're an empath? Have others described you as being "overly sensitive"? Do you become overwhelmed or easily fatigued in large crowds? When you meet strangers in a crowded room, do they begin to tell you intimate details of their lives almost immediately? Do friends routinely monopolize your telephone conversations with their "poor me" stories? Do you begin to feel ill when visiting a friend or relative in a hospital?

These are all common signs associated with being an empath. As an empath, it seems that other people's emotions and even physical sicknesses can become your own. You are like an energetic sponge, soaking up all the emotions around you – both the negative and the positive. Your sensitivity is a gift but left untrained, it can drain you. Remember, we only want and need our own energies.

How can I control my gift? Meditation can help you to learn to control the crown chakra (the energetic center atop your head) so that you do not feel constantly bombarded by others' thoughts, feelings, and physical ailments. Take care to meditate before you leave your home each day so that your chakras and your overall aura are not overextended. Then, before bed, do another meditation: a chakra-cleansing meditation. Neither meditation needs to be longer than 15 minutes, and it can be done while you bathe, leisurely walk the dog, listen to calming music, or just relax.

Another great tip is to use sage as a method of clearing your aura (the energetic field around your body). As always, first set the intention to remove all energies that cling to you and do not serve you. Then, bring the sage smoke around your entire body, first down and then back up, toward the heart and over the head. Let it stay for a bit to absorb those excess energies; then you can back out of the room and open a window to clear the smoke.

If it's not your preference to use sage smoke in your home, you can achieve similar results by using some Epsom or pink Himalayan salts in the bath, or sage soap in the shower. In either case, visualize the salt or soap suds rinsing the excess energies down the drain.

Mother Nature is the ultimate purifier! Spend some time outside, walking barefoot in the grass, hiking through quiet woods, or swimming in the ocean or a natural lake. Water is an amazing clearing tool. Remember, we are mostly made of water, plants are mostly water, and we live on a planet that is mostly water.

Speaking of plants and the planet, try to eat a variety of high-vibrational fruits and vegetables. Physicians and nutritionists tell their patients to eat foods that span "the colors of the rainbow." As an energy healer, I say to eat foods that span the colors of the chakras! These nutritious, high-fiber foods not only cleanse your body, but they also cleanse your energies. The goal is to align your physical body with its perfect auric vibration, like tuning a radio dial to get just the right reception.

If you're feeling drained and could possibly attribute it to your empathic gift, try picturing a helmet on the top of your head that no energies can permeate. Or, envision yourself encased in a mirrored bubble, where others' energies will just bounce off it. You could also visualize a beautiful white light wrapping its way around your body, shielding and healing you.

If you're feeling cloudy and "out of it," envision flowering vines wrapped around your ankles that are deeply rooted in the strong bedrock of Mother Earth. Ask her to ground you. You can picture "flushing" excess energies down the vines and into the Earth, where they will be absorbed.

Remember to take some time for yourself too. A soothing massage or facial can renew both body and soul. And laughter is the best medicine! Watch a funny movie, dance or sing, or just be silly. Your soul will soar. A Reiki session with a certified practitioner will help keep your chakras open and spinning at their optimum vibration.

Holidays Can Be Tough (Guarding And Protecting Your Energy)

The holidays can be an especially tough time for almost every family, and sometimes when there are some very opinionated voices in the mix, it can be difficult to keep the peace. I believe we all have the right to our own beliefs, and it would be nice for family members that are getting together for a celebration to honor those around them. Families can be the hardest to get along with because we are here to learn valuable lessons from each other. Keeping the peace with our family members during holiday gatherings can be full of anxiety and stress, and to many, the sadness of lost loved ones who will not be joining us around the table or at the gathering can be as painful as the day we lost them.

Try to imagine how they are feeling and find only compassion for those who find it difficult to keep things peaceful. Our lives are made up of memories, and when we are missing someone, special emotions can stir, and it's not really about who is gathered, but who is not in the room.

We can feel angry that we no longer have that special person with us. We don't know what is going on inside someone's heart or mind that could be making them behave badly. We need to pull out all our compassion and wisdom to know when to speak and when to hold our tongues.

Try to be as understanding as you can without giving away your own contentment. We need to take care of ourselves first. Keep those who are pulling you into their drama at a distance and send them light and love.

Just remember the Golden Rule: Treat others as we would like to be treated. Look to your heart to find the kindness and compassion for those who do not understand or are missing the tools in their toolbox to recognize pure love without putting restrictions on others. Stay away from the naysayers trying to bring others down so that they may feel better about themselves. Forgive them, Lord, for they know not what they do.

The celebrations that are coming up have beautiful meanings to them. Try to get your guest or hostess focused on the meaning of the holidays instead of themselves and their current situation. Unconditional love is about honoring yourself and others. Be that person that God made you to be and remember that this too shall pass. Keep these words from the Bible in your heart: "Love is patient, Love is kind."

Here are some tips to guarding and protecting your energy while going into any gathering or party during the holidays:

1. First, picture a beautiful white light coming up through the soles of your feet – God's beautiful, healing, white light. The light comes up through the soles of your feet and then, like a ribbon, starts to wrap around your ankles, calves, your legs, stomach, chest and back, shoulders and neck and right up to the top of your head (your crown chakra). This beautiful white light of protection is like a hug from God and a shield from Archangel Michael. Picture this white light while at the same time asking for protection from any hurtful thoughts or feelings coming your way. Ask for only joy and happiness to surround you.

2. Ground your energy before leaving the house, so you feel connected to Mother Earth, becoming centered and relaxed. Picture a beautiful ball of green light starting at the top of your head and coming down into the crown chakra, your forehead, throat, heart, stomach, legs, and arms, and feeling this ball of light releasing any nerves or anxiety that you are feeling down to Mother Earth. The green ball of light continues down through the soles of your feet, going down 12 inches into Mother Earth. You are now grounded.

3. Remember James Billet Freeman's prayer of protection: "The Light of God surrounds me, The Love of God enfolds me, The Power of God protects me, The Presence of God watches over me, For wherever I am, God is!"

Living Spiritually

It's not the easiest thing in the world learning to adjust to any adversities that pop up in our lives. It's going to happen to even the most spiritual people on the planet.

You seem to have it all figured out – do unto others as you would have them do to you. Live your life with intention and have a beautiful and peaceful soul. You know you're a good person who tries to treat others with respect and without judging. You give to charities, and you smile at everyone you meet on the street or in the grocery store. You pay attention to the feelings of friends and family and even people you don't know very well. You pray and meditate, and everything seems to be on an even keel, and then what happens? A life-changing experience shakes your world. An experience you didn't see coming. The loss of a loved one, or a sickness in the family. You get laid off from a job you love. You lose your best friend, or your marriage falls apart. It's happened to all of us. And when you're doing your very best with everything you put out to the world, you start to wonder why? Why would this happen to me? What did I do to deserve this? It's like the song "Why Me Lord."

It's not easy trying to live a more spiritual life, but I can tell you, in the end, it will pay off. Troubles and tribulations happen for a reason – sometimes we can't see the how's or why's, and we may never find out. I can tell you though that how we react to a situation or problem when it does arise can be a great test of who we really are. They are lessons to be learned so our soul can grow to be perfect and expand in every way. Things sometimes happen so that we too can understand what it feels like when difficulties happen to others. We will live a life having more sympathy or compassion for others with similar problems. The sooner we handle situations with an open mind and ask the question "what am I to learn?", the faster the problem or situation can move away from us.

After my mom passed, my siblings and I fell apart from each other – something I never thought would happen – and I sought out the answers as to why. Clients started coming in for readings that had the same situations happening to them, and I knew then how to counsel them with a greater sympathy that I probably would not have felt as deeply if I hadn't been going through the same things myself. I looked to Heaven and said, "I get it, I AM NOT ALONE."

When you feel like something is happening just to you, believe me, it's not. I have learned first-hand that spirit knows what you are going through, and they are trying their very best to shine a light on the situations that we must endure, but they cannot take away the lesson. If you do not handle a situation with grace and receive the lesson, it will come back to you time and time again until you have grown stronger - until no one has the power to take you away from that feeling of peace. That's when you truly know you are living a spiritual life, when you have FAITH in GOD that you are being cared for.

We will not live a complete life of contentment until we return home, which is to Heaven. This is our schoolroom, and we are here to do the learning. It's a journey - what we signed up for before we came down on Earth to live. We picked our family, friends, and lessons beforehand. It's hard to imagine that, but we did. We can't control our situations, but we can control our actions.

Next time you can show your bright light to others by handling yourself with grace and love, you will feel the feeling of contentment, knowing that you have made the right choice for you. Life is full of disappointments but remember the old saying "when one door closes, another will open." Keep living a spiritually-filled life. It's not just for you but for everyone that can see it shining brightly.

Tips On How To Live A More Spiritual Life

At first, a person who wants to live a more spiritual life may seem to some as a person who simply wants to become closer to God and his energy. And, in fact, by living a spiritual life, people do deepen their understanding of God. But because God created us in his own image, we are also deepening our understanding of ourselves. So, by living a more spiritual life, we come to understand God, ourselves, and everyone around us in a more peaceful, compassionate manner.

Our purpose in life is simply to be happy and love one another. It raises our vibration and brings God closer into our lives when we share our happiness and love with others around us. It costs nothing and takes little time to raise your vibration. Here are some of my favorite tips to bring miracles into your everyday lives:

GOALS: Create a goal to work towards, something fun that you want to try, or a trip you want to embark upon. If it's something that might take months or years to achieve, break it down into smaller segments and work on achieving each segment on the way to your final destination. Once you've arrived at your ultimate goal, you will feel a sense of accomplishment and pride.

HUMOR AND FUN: Smile and the world will smile with you! Watch a funny movie, laugh, dance, sing and do something creative. This instantly raises your vibration and will attract more positive experiences.

GRATITUDE: Be thankful for everything. Even when things are not going your way, there is always something to be thankful for, regardless of how small it may be. An attitude of gratitude will bring many blessings your way.

LOVE: Put love first and foremost and at the center of everything that you do. Unconditional love is God's gift to you. Embrace it and spread it around.

FAITH: Have faith that we are never alone in our journey and are always guided from up above.

We are all human and will occasionally stumble. This is all part of the learning process that we are put here on Earth to do. As you set out to live a more spiritual life, take care not to fall victim to scenarios that can lower your vibration, such as:

CONTROL: Things in life will unfold as they were intended to do so, and there will come a time where we've said and done everything in our power to direct the course of a situation. But we do not have control over how things will work out – only in how we react and learn from them. Sometimes you just have to step back and have faith that things will work out the way they were intended to.

MATERIALISM: Energies tend to settle around clutter, and greed is not a loving emotion. If you find that you've accumulated more than you can use, remember to donate to charity or help another person with your abundance. If you feel that you're in a situation of not having enough, remember to be grateful for what you do have and to ask for only what you truly need.

FEAR: Fear is the opposite emotion of love. I think of FEAR as False Evidence Appearing Real. Where love is, fear cannot survive. Ask yourself "What am I truly afraid of? Where does my fear come from? And how can I love and guide myself through it?"

WORRY AND ANXIETY: These emotions will sap your energy and distract you from God and everything else that you should be focusing on instead. It's like rocking in a rocking chair – you're constantly moving but not getting anywhere. Take a deep breath instead and try to refocus your attention.

TOXINS: Processed foods and other unhealthy substances can drain you of vitality and energy. Eat plenty of fruits and vegetables that are the colors of the chakras, drink lots of water, and get enough rest so you will be able to raise your vibrations. Avoid pollutants and other toxic places and get outside in nature whenever possible.

NEGATIVITY: Negative people will dull your vibration and create an unhappy environment around you. Surround yourself instead with people who care for you and support you. Try to turn those negative-nelly's around by sharing your positivity and joy. Keep tabs on your thoughts as well – negative thoughts can bring about negative actions.

So, come on and get happy! Do what brings you joy and try to minimize situations in your life that are stressful. If you do find yourself in a stressful situation, try to look for its positive aspects. Ask yourself: What have I learned from this? Simply by turning the stress into a lesson, you are raising your vibration. Be present, and truly live in the moment.

New Year, New You!

How many of you out there start the new year off making resolutions, fully intending to keep them, then realize just a few weeks into the year that they have fallen by the wayside? I'm sure most of us are guilty of that! So just how do you make those resolutions stick? What can you do to live a more spiritual life full of gratitude?

Recently, I went on a vacation with my family. When on vacation, I always try to find some time for myself to intentionally clear my mind and let spirit do some talking. The only way for spirit to reach us is when we allow our minds to quiet and clear the junk out. I always take an empty journal or notebook with me so when the thoughts or signs come, I can write them down.

I brought my empty book with me in my suitcase as well as a spiritual book that I had been wanting to read. I even let spirit pick the book that they wanted me to read by going over to my bookcase and asking which book I needed to learn from. I put myself in a place where spirit could come through and give messages, almost like doing a meditation.

The message that came through might seem simple to you, but it was my "a-ha moment"! The first message that came to me was the fact that I was trying to get so many things done at one time and that I was scattering from one task to another. I wasn't taking the time to enjoy each and every blessing that was coming my way.

I heard a distinctive voice say "Take a breath. Slow down. You're running through your own life without enjoying any of it the way you should be". Yes! I had been going full-speed without taking a deep breath to enjoy my hard work.

We are spirit, a soul living in a body, a soul that needs to be replenished and well taken care of. When I say spirit, I refer to God, Jesus, angels, spirit guides and all the people that love you unconditionally from the other side.

And when we stop to quiet all the chatter in our mind, those spirits can finally get a word or two in – words that we need to hear.

So, from this day forward, I am taking the time to take that breath, live in that moment, and rejoice being here on Earth at this time I have chosen.

Please take a moment tonight to thank God for the food you are about to eat for giving you the nutrients that your body needs to help it run. Take time to enjoy your life. It goes by too fast, so dream big and then say a prayer. What's meant to be will be, and what doesn't happen probably means it is not the right time or isn't for your higher or greater good.

Make a schedule for yourself that creates time for the people and things that mean the most to you because this is your time on Earth. Live it well.

What a great message from Spirit!

The next message to come through showed me all the blessings that had happened in the past year. Each blessing was special and meaningful to me, but as I rushed to the next task, I had forgotten about the last one that had occurred. It was almost like Facebook's review of the past year!

It never occurred to me to write down all the fantastic things that had happened for me during the year, but I got out my journal and to my surprise, once I started writing, my year seemed amazing to me. When you write down everything you are grateful for, more and more memories start to surface and the more we show that gratitude, the more we start to realize "wow, I couldn't have done this alone"! We realize that we then know that everyone in Heaven is working behind the scenes in our favor, guiding and showing us the way. Even things that didn't happen, we can say "Thank you, God, that they didn't."

We can't always see the big picture, but spirit sure can.

The next message I got was about the upcoming year ahead of us. Do not let worry and fear be our guides, but rather live with love and faith. Know that God trumps all things! We just need to say those prayers – they are really heard. Take the time to make that vision board for yourself and dream big. Write them down so spirit knows exactly where they can step in and give you a little help.

It's the law of attraction! What you can envision, you can make happen. Thoughts are things. What you think becomes your reality. Go for it! What do you have to lose but regret for not living your life to the fullest? Take the plunge and have a great new year!

Creating Goals – Vision Board

Earlier I spoke about New Year's Resolutions, and how difficult it can be to keep them throughout the year. Resolutions can be a good thing if they are not too hard and are attainable. It's when they are so out of reach that they seem daunting, and when this happens, the resolution that had only the best of intentions can go down the drain, leaving you feeling disappointed in yourself.

The key is to keep a positive outlook in everything you do. Start with a goal with which you can see some results in a measured way so that when you make strides, you can actually see the results and know it's working. That way, you feel motivated to keep moving forward.

Goals can be a good thing to have, especially if you take the time to write them down or even create a vision board, which can be both fun and creative. Using some construction paper and pictures, sit and write your goals down on the board. The vision board shows what you would like to come to fruition in the new year. When you take the time to create this board, you are giving your goals energy, because whatever you give your energy to becomes your reality.

It's giving the universe permission to step in and help. It's almost like saying a prayer - ask, and you shall receive. Don't ever be afraid to ask the universe for its help.

A great time to start your vision board is in January at the start of a new year. Create it and hang it up where you can peek at it from time to time and see what's being accomplished and what still needs some more time or energy. The universe only wants what is best for your highest and greatest good, and sometimes it's in God's timing, so be patient.

Be specific on what goals you want to happen. The more specific, the better, so that spirit knows exactly what you have in mind for yourself.

Goals can be anything from losing weight, to career, or to love. Say you want a vacation – putting up a picture of a beach with palm trees swaying gives you a vision — one step at a time, but with a little help from spirit.

Always try to stay positive because things in the physical world can be challenging. Your attitude can be a goal-changer. Be a positive role model, not just for yourself, but for others around you as well. People will see you as a shining light of positivity, and this energy will be contagious and brought back to you. What you give out you receive back.

Keep a high vibrational energy by getting enough sleep, eating as many fruits and vegetables as possible, and staying hydrated. Listen to your favorite uplifting music on the way to work. Surround yourself with positive people during the day, the ones who encourage you to be your best. Everyone has good intentions at the beginning of the year. Try to keep that vibe going through the following months by doing fun projects, leaving time to socialize or just time to relax and be yourself. All spirit wants is for you to live a life filled with joy and laughter and not to be so hard on yourself. If you feel you need support, join a group or take a class with people who have the same goals as yourself.

Another great way to keep intentions in the new year is to start the day with daily affirmations. You can do this before you get out of bed in the morning or while taking a shower. One I like to use and that I find helpful is saying the following affirmation three times: "Healthy am I, Happy and I, Holy am I, and so it is." It's a great affirmation that I learned a long time ago.

You can also make up your own or find another that fits you. Either way, starting your day with positive, happy thoughts is a great way to begin your day and keep yourself focused on a great new year.

Manifestation

Did you ever find yourself wondering why some people seem to have it all, while others seem to lack in abundance or love? This is about manifestation – how to make your dreams come true. Thoughts are things, and what you believe, you will achieve. Those who truly believe they have it all will have it all. The same goes for those who feel lack within their lives.

The reason our beliefs shape our realities is that the universe responds to our energies as if it were a mirror: our thoughts, good or bad, are reflected back to us in the form of situations, people or coincidences. As a funny example, have you ever been on a diet and tried to watch TV? Every ad is for junk food! Yet, if you are not dieting, those ads don't seem to turn up

God only wants the best for us. He and your team of guardian angels, spirit guides and loved ones who have passed on truly want you to make the most of your journey here on Earth in a way that is uniquely fulfilling to you. When you strive toward your ultimate potential, it benefits not only you but also humanity and God. It is a powerful motivator!

Simply writing down or illustrating our goals is a step toward manifestation. I've always kept a vision board for myself. Yours can be simple or more elaborate but should contain images you've envisioned that represent your ideal future. You can cut words and pictures out of magazines and paste them onto poster board to remind yourself of your goals.

Examples might be writing down the word "vacation" with a picture of a tropical destination for a long-overdue getaway, or a graduation cap for completing that college degree you've been putting off, or an image of a happy couple if you're in search of a love relationship.

Try to imagine how you'll feel once you've achieved that goal – the well-earned relief from work as you sink your toes into warm sand, the pride of hanging a college degree on your wall, and the love from a romantic partnership. Emotions help the universe to align itself to meet your goal. At first, I'd suggest selecting one or two goals. Pray or meditate daily on it, with the intention of your goal being in your highest and greatest good. With a daily routine, the thought of that goal as your future reality becomes a habit. Plus, this way you are stating it to the universe and God, which holds you accountable.

You can even incorporate physical elements of your goal into your meditation. For instance, if part of your vacation vision is sinking your feet into the soft sand, you can purchase play sandbox sand, pour some into a dishpan, and sink your feet into it. For the graduation example, choose clothing that shares the school's colors. Your physical body will become used to becoming immersed in that color, so a graduation robe in that color will be a natural progression. If you are looking for a love relationship, physically make room for that special person in your life. Clear out half your closet, sleep on one side of the bed, and make a space for a second set of toiletries on the bathroom vanity. As they say, "fake it 'til you make it." Have fun and be creative!

Try to be specific in your vision too. A humorous example I've heard is one regarding a single woman who wanted "someone who will love me unconditionally." While she did receive unconditional love, it was because a puppy came into her life – not the tall, dark, handsome man for whom she had hoped! The more specific, the better but let the universe surprise you. Oftentimes, we aim too low, and the universe grants us gifts beyond our wildest dreams.

Then, take practical steps toward achieving your goal. For financial abundance, we need to do more than buy a lottery ticket. Remember, God helps those who help themselves. Pray, meditate, send out resumes, network and go on job interviews. Like attracts like, and you'll find, after a while, that the universe mirrors and amplifies your goal. Co-create with God, and your dream job will be far more fulfilling than any lotto payment.

Allow the miracle of manifestation to unfold in its own time. Everything good is worth the wait! If you're feeling antsy, ask the universe for a specific sign or synchronicity that affirms you are working together. This is a miracle unto itself! Keep your eye out for feathers, birds, music and more that have a significant and powerful meaning to you.

How You Can Prepare For The Best Reading

It's so gratifying for me to see my clients reach a place of healing and peace once they learn, with proof from the other side, that their loved ones are still with them in spirit.

There are many ways you can prepare for a mediumship reading, and the more prepared you are, the more in-depth a reading (and healing) you may receive. It's definitely beneficial for you to prepare.

The most important way to prepare is simply to come with an open heart and an open mind. Don't worry; you'll receive specific evidence in abundance that your loved one is thriving on the other side. Your loved ones have so much to say!

And they are so very excited to talk to you. They want you to know, more than anything, that they are still very much alive – they have simply shed their human bodies when they transitioned to Heaven. And they want to communicate their eternal love to you.

Just as you might have had your loved in in attendance during major life events or called them immediately to ask for guidance during trying situations while they were alive, they are now still fully present for you. Think of them, and they're there!

Interestingly, just as we grow as a person, once we've experienced a major life event, our loved ones can also shift and soften after their physical deaths. I once channeled a parent for a client who I described to a "T" – with one exception. In the afterlife, the parent was kind, with a soft personality. After the mediumship reading had ended, the client said to me, "Thank you for saying my father was nice. He wasn't that way in life." Apparently, he had been gruff in life – but after his passing and life review, he softened. He realized his gruffness had only hindered him in life, and so he changed. Self-improvement can happen on either side of the spirit realm.

I find that those who were good communicators in life are excellent communicators in the afterlife too. Extroverts are outgoing, even in spirit. These spirits are the ones who provide ample and specific evidence of their time on Earth and their relationship to the client. They know your thoughts and what transpires throughout your day.

Often the spirit will tell me how he or she passed; by disease, unexpectedly, by accident. I'll even learn which disease, what occurrence, or what accident. They'll tell me their major life moments, from childhood until their passing. I'll learn how many siblings they had, their school or work careers, if they married and had children or even grandchildren. I might not get a full name, but I may get initials. And I'll get confirmation, in symbols or signs, that they were there with you for important experiences, like attending or acknowledging major life events.

Because I am clairvoyant, I can actually see the loved one standing beside you. He or she may not come through in spirit how they last appeared in life. They may be careful to appear in a way that you might recognize at first, and they change their appearance to reflect when and how they felt best in life. If they served in the military and strongly identified with that, they may appear in uniform. If a spirit passed as a child, that individual might appear fully grown now.

I know that most of my clients come into a reading hoping to connect with a particular loved one who has passed. If a client comes in and specifically asks for someone special, often they'll come right through immediately. But if they don't, there are ways in which I may inquire about them.

If they passed recently from a long, draining illness, or unexpectedly and suddenly, they may need time to get their bearings in the spirit world and build their energy enough to communicate. Another loved one may shepherd them through and communicate on their behalf, or we may learn that they are still adjusting and healing on the other side, and to try later, once they've built their energetic strength.

It truly is my pleasure and life's purpose to bring you news of your loved one's well-being in Heaven. I consider mediumship my God-given gift, and it is my sacred honor to share it with you.

Group Or Private Reading?

A demonstration or gallery reading is where a large group of people gather in hopes of receiving a message from the medium who's doing the demonstration. These gallery events can vary from one to the next, as each medium has his or her own style and personality and ways that they put the demonstrations together.

I know that when I put on an event, it is with the intention of bringing a group together in a space where they feel safe to receive a message. It's also a great platform to see a particular medium's work in action. In a group setting like this, not everyone will receive a personal message, but, hopefully, the event will leave everyone with the feeling and knowing that love never dies, it is eternal and everlasting, and there is proof that our loved ones are always next to us in our everyday lives.

Evidential mediumship is when a medium can give you evidence or proof that the communicator (your loved one) is passing on to him or her to give to you. Evidential information may include such things as their name and relationship, the color of their eyes, how they passed, what were their hobbies while here on Earth, and, most importantly, what is the message that comes from their heart to you. Sometimes they will offer guidance to what is going on in your life; or if there are celebrations or birthdays that are around the time of the event, they want to acknowledge them and let you know they were there celebrating with you.

This evidence is some of what you may receive either in a demonstration setting or a private reading.

The biggest difference in the two settings is that you are not guaranteed a personal message at a demonstration or gallery. That doesn't mean that your loved ones didn't show up at the event because, believe me, there is someone for everyone at each event I have ever done. It just means there is only so much time at each event, and each medium tries to give as many messages as time allows.

I always start off my events or readings by saying a prayer and asking your loved ones to join us. I continue by telling everyone a little bit about myself and how I work with my gift; this allows the energy in the room to blend. The best reading you will receive is if everyone's energy has melded together and opened the lines of communication. I always explain the fact that demonstrations do not take the place of a private reading, where it's just you, me, and spirit (your loved ones).

A private reading is a time to connect for 45-60 minutes, with the focus on you and your loved ones who have passed before you, or even a family pet that might like to come through. Loved ones in heaven, or even yourself, may have a regret, or another deep hurt that can be healed more comfortably through a private conversation or setting.

Mediumship work is just that: healing for both sides. A good medium knows how to go about giving sensitive information that may come through in a group setting, but sometimes it's just not the place to have a full conversation. A private reading gives you the chance to sit and talk things over in a quiet setting, to bring forth that conversation so that healing can take place.

Some mediums, like myself, offer spiritual counseling and can offer ways to learn from these sensitive subjects in a safe, caring environment.

Events are amazing, and private readings are just as amazing! It just depends on whether you need that one-on-one conversation with your loved one on the other side, or if you just want to see what receiving messages is all about.

My suggestion if you're unsure which way is best for you would be to go to a demonstration first. If you're not sure how you feel about receiving a message, then go and watch the medium giving the messages; if you trust what you are hearing and seeing, then make an appointment for a private reading. If you feel like you would like a one-on-one, ask around or ask friends who they have been to until you find someone you might be comfortable with.

Finding the right medium for you will help your messages come through loud and clear.

The Demonstrating Medium

One way a medium can share her gift is in front of a large crowd waiting to hear from their loved ones and hoping they will be the receiver of a message. This is done as a demonstration or what some call a gallery. All eyes are upon the medium as they enter and become the center of attention. Most mediums will prefer doing one-to-one readings while others enjoy demonstrating more.

The demonstrating medium must be confident when working with spirit and large audiences of people at the same time; becoming the entertainer of sorts, even though the work is serious and can change how others view Heaven and dying. The demonstrating medium will need to know when to be sad and show sympathy as the story unfolds of how this person left the Earth plane, and to also know when to raise the vibration of the audience by bringing joy and laughter from the spirit world. Most audience members do attend to witness the miracle of communicating with the other side, while others are skeptics or just curious to see how this unfolds. A good medium will make the connection seem effortless while bringing forth the evidential proof of life after death.

The communicator on the other side will provide vital details; how they lived, died and their attributes, personality and unique quirks that they had on this side of life, all in the hopes that you will recognize them as you knew them on this side of life. It really is like having a three-way conversation; FROM SPIRIT, THROUGH SPIRIT, TO SPIRIT. The perfect connection will leave the medium and the recipient feeling exhilarated. It is so gratifying to see the love and healing that a message can bring.

There are two ways in which a medium can bring a message forth in a gallery - direct and indirect. The indirect choice is allowing spirit to pick who is going to step forward and delivering the details of this spirit to an open crowd; therefore, finding the recipient of the message. The direct method is used when the medium is pulled to a person in the audience and permission is given by that person to work with them. It's like giving permission to the spirit world to start a conversation. This always starts off with "I feel like I am with you, would you like a message?" The direct method always takes less time than the indirect method, but the indirect method can bring an audience together and make them all feel included in the process. I have found both ways work equally well.

The role of the demonstrating medium is to represent the spirit world, presenting the information that is coming through while intriguing the audience at the same time. It is a great responsibility.

The medium has done their job well if she has inspired, fascinated, and kept the crowd enthralled and filled with wonder, while at the same time keeping it genuine and trustworthy, leaving the audience feeling the souls of the loved ones who have come through with no doubt that life continues. If the messages were given with compassion and confidence, the medium has done their job well.

Most mediums need to know to just be yourself, that's the best we can do. Share your own personal stories and make your audience laugh and feel relaxed in your presence. If you attend a gallery or event, come with an open heart and mind and enjoy being in the presence of miracles (in the form of messages). The spirit world is amazing!

Dealing With Skeptics

Skeptics are everywhere, and sometimes it can be difficult to deal with the person who books an appointment with you and then says flat out "I don't believe."

I handle the situation a lot different than I used to. When doing an event people would actually come up to me and tell me "I am here just to watch, I don't believe in Mediums." I won't lie - it used to make me nervous that someone would call for a reading and tell me over the phone "I don't really believe, but I would like to see what you have to say." No pressure there! But I have learned to deal with a skeptic in a totally different manner these days. In fact, when I asked spirit why these people kept coming to me I heard, "well it's easy to give a reading to someone who loves what you do and never questions you, but the people we need to reach are the ones that do not believe there is life after death, or have that big empty space in their heart because they have lost someone close and they just don't know if there is anymore after this world".

They are the ones who see death as an ending instead of a new beginning. They feel the absence of their loved one's physical bodies being with them and might think that there truly is an ending. They miss hearing their laughter or listening to their stories and advice or sitting down and having a cup of tea together. But life does go on, just in a different place, but really very much the same.

Our loved ones keep their traits and personalities just like when they were here and sometimes maybe even hold on to a regret that they have now that they can see the bigger picture since being in Heaven and having that life review. They go through a life review on the other side, not to be judged but to see where they could have improved or where they could have shown more compassion or love. They have regrets just like we do.

Many spirits come to me with these regrets and want to say they are sorry for their mistakes, and now with this new awareness, they know it's always about the love that we show to others while we are here, how much we loved and forgave others.

Skeptics play an important role in my job as a Medium because when skeptics see and hear for themselves the messages and memories that are still in their thoughts and prayers, it opens up a brand-new world for them. It actually starts a new beginning of seeing and believing in a different way than before. So that voice from up above revealed to me these are the people we need to reach out to.

My outlook is: I can't make anyone a believer, but I can give you evidence if you come to a reading or event with an open heart and mind. I can't speak for other mediums, but it took a while for me to realize that everyone doesn't come from the same background of believing, and it's my job to share with them that Heaven is for real and their loved ones are safe and sound and really not that far away.

What Do Your Loved Ones Need You To Know?

Here's what I've heard from Heaven:

LOVE NEVER DIES

One day I was putting fresh roses in a vase and as I bent down to smell one of the roses I heard the voice of my father-in-law asking me to bring a rose to his wife here on Earth, as it was her birthday dinner that same evening. Then these words started coming to me, flowing. I grabbed a piece of paper and continued to write them down as fast as they came. Here are those words:

> Your loved one
> Still with you
> From up above,
> Watching and caring
> From a place of love.
> They never leave you –
> Just look up
> Where your eyes
> Will meet
> Full of love.
> Life goes on but love never dies.
> And your loved one
> Will meet you
> On the other side.

Till we meet again
Know that I am there,
Protecting and guiding
With Love
That's always there.
Your love.

When I looked down at the piece of paper, this beautiful poem was formed. I didn't need to change a word.

I looked up and assured my father-in-law that I would not only give these beautiful sentiments to his wife that was missing him but would also bring her some beautiful roses that night.

I often use these words in a guided meditation that I bring groups through at the end of an event. I add these words from an unknown author.

They send you these thoughts:
I give you this one
Thought to keep
I am with you still –
I do not sleep
I am a thousand winds
That blow
I am the diamond
Glints on snow
I am the sunlight on
Ripened grain
I am the
Gentle autumn rain
When you awaken
In the morning's hush
I am the
Sweet, uplifting rush
Of quiet birds
In circled flight
I am the soft

Stars that shine
At night
Do not think of me as gone
I am with you
Still in each new dawn

So know in your heart that your loved one lives on, never dies, is everlasting and they will never leave you. And if you listen closely you might hear them whisper:

Although we are apart
My spirit will live on
There within your heart
Hold me close
Know that I hear your thoughts and prayers.
With Love
Your Love

What God Wants You To Know

One day as I sat typing at my desk and I was feeling down-in-the-dumps, I started to hear that familiar voice of God speak to me. As he spoke, I wrote down the words that were forming. God asked me to share:

"YOU ARE ENOUGH"
God washed my tears away today
I didn't ask
I didn't need to
I realized everything I do
I do because I am me
And I am Enough
Enough to be loved
And to love with a kind heart
Enough to feel what
Hurt feels like
Enough to feel sympathy
Even for the person
Who hurt me
Sometimes when life
Seems rough
I need to know
I am Enough
Things can tend to get rough
On this rocky road we call life
But there within my heart
I hear "you are Enough"

Beautiful in every way
Every day
You are Enough
-GOD-

So please take these words and keep them there within your heart, for you are loved every day in every way.

About The Author

Bonnie Page is rapidly becoming one of New England's most exciting psychic mediums! Connecting to private clients with integrity and compassion, Bonnie has a gentle, loving, and humorous approach to her gift of spirit communication.

A born medium with conscious memories of spirit communication since the age of four, Bonnie has developed her talents to become a gifted, evidential medium. In 2014 Bonnie heard the voice of God, who instructed her to make her gift her full-time profession. She opened the "Messages From Heaven Healing And Learning Center" where she delivers both private and group messages by appointment.

Bonnie truly has a gift for teaching! She is a Reiki Master/Teacher/ New Age Speaker. She offers classes aimed at helping others to build their own intuitive skills, metaphysical modalities, and New Age thought at her studio and schools and colleges throughout New England. She teaches at the prestigious Lily Dale Assembly in Lily Dale, New York. She has become one of the most sought-after demonstrating mediums, gifting large audiences with insights from the afterlife in local ballrooms, expos and function facilities.

Bonnie currently has her own television show on Leominster TV called "The Medium Next Door" and also writes a weekly newspaper column called "Ask The Psychic."

Today, Bonnie is happy to share her gift with others. She feels inspired to help to do God's work by comforting those who need to hear from their loved ones on the other side. Her compassion, wisdom, sense of humor and calming nature allows her clients to feel comfortable and at ease while receiving evidential proof that their departed loved ones are always around them and that their spirit is eternal.

For more information about Bonnie, please visit www.bonniepagemedium.com.

CONTACT BONNIE PAGE:
Website: www.bonniepagemedium.com
CALL OR E-MAIL:
Phone: (978) 297-9790
E-Mail: bonniepage@verizon.net
MORE WAYS TO CONNECT:
Facebook: www.facebook.com/MediumBonniePage
Instagram: Instagram.com (Mediumbonniepage)

Printed in the United States
By Bookmasters